D0078470

SIMONE WEIL

WOMEN OF IDEAS

Series Editor: Liz Stanley
Editorial Board: Cynthia Enloe and Dale Spender

This series consists of short study guides designed to introduce readers to the life, times and work of key women of ideas. The emphasis is very much on the ideas of these women and the political and intellectual circumstances in which their work has been formulated and presented.

The women featured are both contemporary and historical thinkers from a range of disciplines including sociology, economics, psychoanalysis, philosophy, anthropology, history and politics. The series aims to: provide succinct introductions to the ideas of women who have been recognized as major theorists; make the work of major women of ideas accessible to students as well as to the general reader; and appraise and reappraise the work of neglected women of ideas and give them a wider profile.

Each book provides a full bibliography of its subject's writings (where they are easily available) so that readers can continue their study using primary sources.

Books in the series include:

Eleanor Rathbone
Johanna Alberti

Simone de Beauvoir
Mary Evans

Christine Delphy
Stevi Jackson

Adrienne Rich
Liz Yorke

Simone Weil
Christopher Frost and Rebecca Bell-Metereau

SIMONE WEIL

On Politics, Religion and Society

FROST, CHRISTOPHER J., 1953–

*Christopher Frost and
Rebecca Bell-Metereau*

SAGE Publications
London • Thousand Oaks • New Delhi

32430
. W474
F76
1998

© Christopher Frost and Rebecca Bell-Metereau 1998

First published 1998

All rights reserved. No part of this publication may be reproduced,
stored in a retrieval system, transmitted or utilized in any form or by any
means, electronic, mechanical, photocopying, recording or otherwise,
without permission in writing from the Publishers.

 SAGE Publications Ltd
6 Bonhill Street
London EC2A 4PU

SAGE Publications Inc
2455 Teller Road
Thousand Oaks, California 91320

SAGE Publications India Pvt Ltd
32, M-Block Market
Greater Kailash – I
New Delhi 110 048

British Library Cataloguing in Publication data

A catalogue record for this book is
available from the British Library.

ISBN 0 8039 7862 6
ISBN 0 8039 7863 4 (pbk)

Library of Congress catalog card number 97-062308

Typeset by M Rules
Printed in Great Britain by Biddles Ltd, Guildford, Surrey

For
Our Students (of ideas)
and especially for
Shaela Jaid

JAN 2 4 2001

Contents

Preface

This series introduces readers to the life, times and work of key 'women of ideas' whose work has influenced people and helped change the times in which they lived. Some people might claim that there are few significant women thinkers. However, a litany of the women whose work is discussed in the first titles to be published gives the lie to this: Simone de Beauvoir, Zora Neale Hurston, Simone Weil, Olive Schreiner, Hannah Arendt, Eleanor Rathbone, Christine Delphy, Adrienne Rich, Audre Lorde, to be followed by Rosa Luxemburg, Melanie Klein, Mary Wollstonecraft, Andrea Dworkin and Catherine MacKinnon, Margaret Mead, Charlotte Perkins Gilman, Hélène Cixous, Luce Irigaray and Julia Kristeva, Alexandra Kollontai, and others of a similar stature.

All readers will want to add their own women of ideas to this list – which proves the point. There *are* major bodies of ideas and theories which women have originated; there *are* significant women thinkers; but women's intellectual work, like women's other work, is not taken so seriously nor evaluated so highly as men's. It may be men's perceptions of originality and importance which have shaped the definition and evaluation of women's work, but this does not constitute (nor is there any reason to regard it as) a definitive or universal standard. *Women of Ideas* exists to help change such perceptions, by taking women's past and present production of ideas seriously, and by introducing them to a wide new audience. *Women of Ideas* titles include women whose work is well-known from both the past and the present, and also those unfamiliar to modern readers although renowned among their contemporaries. The aim is to make their work accessible by drawing out of what is a frequently diverse and complex body of writing the central ideas and key themes, not least by locating these in relation to the intellectual, political and personal milieux in which this work originated.

Do women of ideas have 'another voice', one distinctive and different from that of men of ideas? or is this an essentialist claim and are ideas at basis unsexed? Certainly women's ideas are differently positioned with regard to their perception and evaluation. It is still a case of women having to be twice as good to be seen as half as good as men, for the apparatus of knowledge/power is configured in ways which do not readily accord women and their work the same status as that of men. However, this does not necessarily mean either that the ideas produced by women are significantly different in kind or, even if they presently are, that this is anything other than the product of the workings of social systems which systematically differentiate between the sexes, with such differences disappearing in an equal and just society. *Women of Ideas* is, among other things, a means of standing back and taking the longer view on such questions, with the series as a whole constituting one of the means of evaluating the 'difference debates', as its authors explore the contributions made by the particular women of ideas that individual titles focus upon.

Popularly, ideas are treated as the product of 'genius', of individual minds inventing what is startlingly original – and absolutely unique to them. However, within feminist thought a different approach is taken, seeing ideas as social products rather than uniquely individual ones, as collective thoughts albeit uttered in the distinctive voices of particular individuals. Here there is a recognition that ideas have a 'historical moment' when they assume their greatest significance – and that 'significance' is neither transhistorical nor transnational, but is rather temporally and culturally specific, so that the 'great ideas' of one time and place can seem commonplace or ridiculous in others. Here too the cyclical and social nature of the life of ideas is recognized, in which 'new' ideas may in fact be 'old' ones in up-to-date language and expression. And, perhaps most importantly for the *Women of Ideas* series, there is also a recognition of the frequently *gendered* basis of the judgements of the 'significance' and 'importance' of ideas and bodies of work.

The title of the series is taken from Dale Spender's (1982) *Women of Ideas, and What Men have Done to Them.* 'What men have done to them' is shorthand for a complex process in which bodies of ideas 'vanish', not so much by being deliberately suppressed (although this has happened) as by being trivialized, misrepresented, excluded from the canon of what is deemed good, significant, great. In addition to these gatekeeping processes, there are other broader factors at work. Times change, intellectual fashion changes also. One product of this is the often very different interpretation and understanding of bodies of ideas over time: when looked at from different – unsympathetic – viewpoints, then dramatic shifts in the representation of these can occur. Such shifts in intellectual fashion sometimes occur in their own right, while at other times they are related to wider social, economic and political changes in the world. Wars, the expansion and then contraction of colonialism, revolutions, all have had an effect on what people think, how ideas are interpreted and related to, which ideas are seen as important and which outmoded.

'Women of ideas' of course need not necessarily position themselves as feminists nor prioritize concern with gender. The terms 'feminist' and 'woman' are by no means to be collapsed, but they are not to be treated as binaries either. Some major female thinkers focus on the human condition in order to rethink the nature of reality and thus of 'knowledge'. In doing so they also reposition the nature of ideas. Each of the women featured has produced ideas towards that greater whole which is a more comprehensive rethinking of the nature of knowledge. These women have produced ideas which form bodies of systematic thought, as they have pursued trains of thought over the course of their individual lives. This is not to suggest that such ideas give expression to a 'universal essence' in the way Plato proposed. It is instead to reject rigidly dividing 'realist' from 'idealist' from 'materialist', recognizing that aspects of these supposedly categorical distinctions can be brought together to illuminate the extraordinarily complex and fascinating process by which ideas are produced and reproduced in particular intellectual, cultural and historical contexts.

The *Women of Ideas* series is, then, concerned with the 'history of ideas'. It recognizes the importance of the 'particular voice' as well as the shared context; it insists on the relevance of the thinker as well as that which is thought. It is concerned with individuals in their relation to wider collectivities and contexts, and it focuses upon the role of particular women of ideas without 'personifying' or individualizing the processes by which ideas are shaped, produced, changed. It emphasizes that this is a history of *'mentalités collectives'*, recognizing the continuum between the everyday and the elite, between 'common sense' and 'high theory'. Ideas have most meaning in their use, in the way they influence other minds and wider social processes, something which occurs by challenging and changing patterns of understanding. As well as looking at the impact of particular women of ideas, the series brings their work to a wider audience, to encourage a greater understanding of the contribution of these women to the way that we *do* think – and also the way that we perhaps *should* think – about knowledge and the human condition.

Liz Stanley

Acknowledgements

We would like to thank the many people who have helped to produce this book. Kathryn Minyard Frost, Ginger R. Jones, Susan Hanson, Georgeanne Smith and Jean-Pierre Metereau read drafts of the manuscript and offered valuable suggestions. Tara Downer devoted numerous hours to typing and editing the manuscript, and contributing to the bibliography. Liz Stanley and Sage external readers read an initial draft and provided helpful comments. Orlo Strunk, friend and mentor, provided access to his unpublished anthology of Weil's work and continued our discussion of Weil, a conversation that now spans two decades. Where we succeed in conveying Simone Weil's work and life with clarity, we have these people to thank.

Christopher Frost
Rebecca Bell-Metereau

Introduction to Simone Weil

The framework

Contemporary scholars from many academic disciplines are beginning to agree on at least one thing: something called 'reality' does not simply impinge upon the senses of a passive human being; rather, people are actively involved in the quest for meaning. Of course, people perceive 'reality' and 'meaning' differently, and one crucial way in which people differ is in the intensity, diversity and accuracy of their 'readings' of reality.

The philosopher Simone Weil was someone for whom life was a struggle and for whom the task of clarifying her perceptions of reality and meaning was an ongoing one. A reviewer of her *Notebooks* commented, describing her journal entries, that the 'struggle they depict is so desperate, the suffering they reveal is so intense, the intellectual demands they make are so severe that few readers will be equal to the conditions which Simone Weil laid down for a "reading" of life and reality.' In fact parts of Weil's work are so challenging and idiosyncratic that their meaning eludes many readers. In selecting especially compelling excerpts from Weil's writings, placing them in their historical and cultural context, and presenting them in a thematic format, the aim of this book is to make Weil's thought more accessible to readers interested in the variety of fields addressed in her work.

Simone Weil presents a challenge to those who write about her, because her work, thought and life constitute a relatively seamless organic whole. Because contradictory statements and polarities characterize her life, however, delineating her work and her place in the corpus of intellectual writing is not easy. Some authors writing about Weil organize her work into neat packages according to discipline, while others attempt a more holistic or impressionistic portrait, often organized along chronological lines. Both of these methods obscure the structural organization of Weil's thought. In this book, we have made every effort to allow Simone Weil to speak for herself – to speak in her own voice.

The metaphor of 'voice' is now closely identified with feminist ideas, and Weil certainly has much in common with a number of other women of ideas. Because the emphasis throughout her life was on equality rather than gender, however, she did not explicitly define herself as a feminist. Judith Gregory comments that, when she read Robert Coles's book on Simone Weil, she was struck most by the idea that neither Weil nor Coles 'seemed to have any feminist consciousness' (Gregory, 1990, p. 369). Weil was definitely not a self-proclaimed feminist, but then she did not claim to be a member of *any* group. Moreover, during the period between the world wars in which Weil lived, issues of survival were taking precedence over issues of identity, and she occupied much of her time in coordinating political worker movements, addressing citizen responses to war and oppression, and finally in determining the spiritual nature of her entire ethical system. While it is true that she felt a pressing need to sort out her spiritual life at the expense of most other planes of existence, she never lost her commitment to political and social equality. The issue of gender, then, was definitely subsumed under larger problems of inequality and injustice, not only for Weil but for many women of her era.

Long before postmodern or deconstructionist ideas were current, Weil theorized about language and the social construction of ethics, social interaction and modes of organization and power politics. According to Mark Taylor, 'as social activist, as educational theorist, and as philosopher of history, Simone Weil championed those passive victims whose goodness history had rewarded with silence. Hers was a defeated, anonymous and vanished constituency: those peoples, simply, who had lost, as they nearly always would in this world, and whose losing meant neglect or calumny in the official chronicles of their conquerors' (Taylor, 1973, p. 451).

Like many women intellectuals and social theorists during the early part of the twentieth century, Weil worked in relative isolation, often having men as her closest allies and mentors. And like many other women of ideas, she also discovered that she could not find a perfect fit with any specific organization, cause or thinker. Thus she often resorted to analysing situations and circumstances from a distance, and, as World War II approached, she was increasingly restricted by gender, ill health and ethnic origin (her family was Jewish) from participating directly in the kind of action and selfless heroism she longed to perform to alleviate the suffering of others. While this distant vantage point may be viewed as a liability, it may also be a source of her singular vision.

Whether to focus on Weil's outsider status or her place within larger groups is an important issue. Often the interpretation of ideas has focused on single theorists as isolated individuals, looking at the influences that shaped each person and made the work unique. An alternative to this 'great person in history' approach is to see individuals within their socio-cultural context. A large amount of writing about Simone Weil has portrayed her primarily as an outcast, as a figure on the margins of society and its conventional groupings. While this portrait certainly captures an important feature of Weil, it fails to convey the broader portrait: many people in this era were expatriates or outcasts, were caught in the grips of profound ethical dilemmas, and were struggling with concepts of individual versus collective identity. These pivotal issues surface in Weil's work, but they are definitive intellectual and political issues for an era as well.

Another issue is whether to focus on Weil as a philosopher, or whether to emphasize the more synthetic and integrative aspects of her thinking. Simone Weil's work is, we believe, best approached from an interdisciplinary, integrative perspective. Her writings cover terrain bounded by the traditional fields of philosophy, science, mathematics, religion, sociology, literature, art, psychology and political science. Thus, her work transcends the artificial boundaries of academic disciplines as she reaches towards a truly holistic system of social thought.

Weil's work is particularly interesting in its attempts to fill the gap between theory and its application to disenfranchised groups. One of the key issues discussed in contemporary feminist theory is whether the ethics systems developed by the patriarchal philosophical tradition are 'inadequate to many intimate, unequal, unchosen particular relationships and therefore exclusive or deforming of much of the matter of social life' (Walker, 1992, p. 25). Traditional Western philosophy's focus on equality and autonomy ignores much of the life experience of women, 'since women's socially assigned responsibilities have so often precisely to do with just these kinds of [unequal and dependent] relations, and with many forms of "caring labor" that sustain them' (ibid.). But the critique is more fundamental than simply focusing on the mainstream of theoretical work. 'Doing theory' is described as 'just a bonding ritual for academic or educationally privileged feminist women' by Lugones and Spelman (1983, p. 579), because of the exclusiveness of the language used and the relatively privileged lives of those in the academy, contrasted with those members of outcast groups.

Kathryn Pyne Addelson observes that unless philosophers maintain a keen sense of the social institutions and customs that form, and are justified by, philosophical theories, the enshrining of theories themselves may constitute part of 'the processes and the preservation of systematic gender, age, class, and race divisions' (Addelson, 1987, p. 105).

Certainly Simone Weil was concerned, indeed preoccupied, with this problem of how one could engage all classes and groups in the kinds of philosophical questions usually reserved for an intellectual and economic elite. She was firm in her conviction that everybody is capable of engaging in a moral dialogue, and that an integral part of that dialogue is considering the material circumstances of the participants in it. She began trying to live out her principles in practice while she was still a student, when lecturing in the Social Education Group in the municipal school in the rue Falguière in Paris. David McClellan observes that despite her sincere desire to bring philosophy to the masses, she may not have been personally effective in doing so: 'Weil's lectures there were less successful than those of her friends: although the railway workers liked her well enough, her ideas were often too bold and paradoxical' (McClellan, 1990, pp. 20–1). Also, as a lecturer Weil had little ability to interest listeners, and she often spoke quickly, in monotone, as if to herself. However, if the content and the delivery of her ideas inhibited easy comprehension, the written form her ideas took presented even more problems for an audience.

A major difficulty in interpreting Simone Weil's work arises from the method – or lack of method – of its publication. Although Weil wished desperately to convey her message to others, she chose to express herself primarily in essays, thoughts jotted in notebooks, and reflections recorded in personal journals. Weil's method of writing is similar to that of many women writers, but it may also be a result of her early work with her teacher at the Lycée Henri IV, Alain (Emile-Auguste Chartier), whose primary teaching method was to have students explore topics in brief, focused essays. Weil takes the process a step further in her notebooks, jotting down slivers of insight in brief, fragmented, shorthand form. Such an expressive format runs counter to a more conventional path to publication, wherein an author's ideas are ordered by topic or theme, rendering them more or less as a whole. Thus, Weil's extended audience encounters her ideas only after her death and generally in incomplete bits and pieces, often organized by others, with little sense of the development of these themes within the broader whole. By organizing her work thematically in this volume, and by relating such themes to the broader ideational structure of her thinking, we hope to convey the larger pattern of her life and work, thereby conveying the essential unity of her vision.

The course we have charted in this book navigates between two polarities in introducing Weil. On the one hand, many collections have presented readers with relatively undigested snippets that lacked any context to assist in understanding. On the other, a good few interpretations are considerably overzealous in rendering, rephrasing and appropriating her work, thereby skewing the reader's understanding according to the particular author's vision. In steering between these, we alternate between presenting our analysis and providing extensive quotations in Weil's own voice, without commentary. The latter form may take more effort to interpret, but it has the benefit of allowing the reader to make connections that are not mediated by another reader or author. Obviously the very fact that quotations have been selected according to thematic concerns represents some interpretation of the material, but the use of extended quotations in thematically organized chapters is intended to allow readers to sample Weil's thought at first hand. In other passages Weil's ideas are analysed, but these interpretations are suggestive rather than prescriptive: the comments and analysis are intended to provoke ideas for further exploration, rather than serve as conclusions for closure. Weil herself demonstrated an amazing ability to counter her own ideas with dialectic alternatives, and she changed her mind about a number of issues. We delineate how some of these changes took place, thereby demonstrating the continuity and subtlety of Weil's evolving views on such complex issues as human nature, good and evil, divinity and truth.

The biographical context

Simone Weil's early life suggested a future of prestige, even luxury, but she intentionally rejected the path of privilege, choosing instead the way of struggle and self-sacrifice. The contrast between her upper middle-class upbringing and the life of poverty she chose causes much confusion in understanding Weil's life. Her choice seems especially inexplicable when contrasted with the capitalistic notion of individuals who rise from poverty and achieve wealth, thus overcoming the obstacles of the class in which they were born. How does one go about understanding a person who diverges so greatly from these social norms?

Susanne Langer has proposed one solution, based on an interpretation of 'understanding', which she sees as 'more like *having a new experience* than like entertaining a new proposition' (Langer, 1942, p. 263; our emphasis). In other words, one does not try to explain a person's life, an approach that often ends up explaining away that life; instead, the aim is to enter the other's world and, insofar as possible, to see and experience it as the other person might.

It is in this specific sense of *understanding* that we approach Simone Weil's life and work. The goal is to explore Weil's readings of reality, an approach which implies vicariously experiencing the world as Weil did, at least to the extent that one can ever enter the consciousness of another. She conveys her sense that she was misunderstood, even by those who had the benefit of knowing her (and perhaps especially so by those who knew her personally), in a letter to her mother written only five weeks before her death in 1943:

> Darling M., you think I have something to give. That is badly expressed. But I too have a sort of growing inner certainty that there is a deposit of pure gold in me which ought to be passed on. The trouble is that I am more and more convinced . . . that there is no one to receive it. . . . It's a dense mass. What gets added to it is of a piece with the rest. . . . I can't parcel it out into little pieces.
>
> It would require an effort to come to terms with it. And making an effort is so tiring!
>
> Some people feel vaguely that there is something there. But they content themselves with uttering a few eulogistic epithets about my intelligence and that completely satisfies their conscience. Then they listen to me or read me with the same fleeting attention they give everything else, taking each little fragment of an idea as it comes along and making a definitive mental decision: 'I agree with this,' 'I don't agree with that. . . .' They conclude: 'It's very interesting,' and then go on to something else. They haven't tired themselves. (Weil, 1978, pp. 1–2)

Readers may tire as they tackle Simone Weil's work because of the difficulty of her thought and the intellectual demands that she makes, but they are more often likely to be fatigued and confused by the presentation of her life and work by biographers and critics offering biographical 'portraits'. And although dismissals and criticisms frequently express extreme views of what kind of woman and thinker Weil was, it may well be her admirers who have most skewed her work and life. For example, to explain her apparent anorexia or her irascibility by calling her a saint, as T. S. Eliot did, neither satisfies the critics, nor promotes a greater understanding of these aspects of her life and character (Eliot, in Weil, 1952, p. vi).

To describe Simone Adolphine Weil, one might naturally begin with her birth in Paris on 3 February 1909, to Selma Reinherz Weil (1872–1955) and Bernard Weil (1879–1965). Born a month prematurely, Weil was never a robust child, but she grew reasonably well at first. When in August 1909 her mother had appendicitis, she attempted to continue nursing her child, but the baby began to lose weight. At sixteen months she refused to be fed, and she grew so weak that she had to be fed strained solids through a bottle with holes punched in the nipple (Pétrement, 1976, p. 7). As an adult, Weil was to remark that being deprived of her mother's milk explained why she was 'so incomplete a being', and she was later to write, before her death in London, 'I prefer having a mother like mine (not to mention my father . . .) despite the bad milk' (Fiori, 1989, p. 14).

From the time of her birth on, two dominant motifs appear in Weil's self-presentation – food and gender – and many aspects of her life may be understood in reference to her conflicted attitude toward these themes. Simone Weil's peculiar relationship to food may also be traced to her birth placement and gender. Her parents' treatment of her older brother André influenced her life, and her relationship with him shaped her thinking in a number of ways. Food was an issue for both children; she and her brother went from house to house in Jullouville in 1914, telling people that they were dying of hunger because their parents would not feed them. In response, they received food, candies and sweets from neighbours – much to the mortification of their parents. This was a household in which food carried great significance, and Weil's mother continually tried to get her daughter to eat more as she began to weigh less and less. Throughout her life, Weil would return to images of food, feeding and sustenance as a metaphor for emotional satisfaction or deprivation; when her life turned in an explicitly spiritual direction, the metaphor of eating was central. Weil's exaggerated attention to food may have been reinforced by her family's suspicion of physicality. For instance, biographical accounts of the family describe André and Simone Weil as young children developing a fear of microbes and therefore an aversion to embracing or kissing, as a result of the family's exaggerated fear of contracting an illness from another person. Certainly in

French society, where hand-shaking among strangers and kisses on the cheek among acquaintances are *de rigueur*, this physical standoffishness must have caused offence on more than one occasion.

Such accounts of the children's activities indicate that the home life of the Weils was in no way conventional. Although the Weils lived comfortably on money made by the father's medical practice, they were hardly a typical bourgeois French family. Their unconventional style may be attributed in large part to the influence of Selma Reinherz Weil. She came from a wealthy intellectual background, growing up in a household with fourteen servants in which famous artists visited regularly, often coming in the afternoon and staying until the next morning. As a young woman, she had wanted to study medicine, but her father did not allow this, a situation which might have contributed to her nascent feminism.

Bernard Weil was born in Alsace and, although his family moved to Paris, his mother remained an outsider: she never learned to speak French and she continued to practise orthodox Judaism. Bernard Weil did not continue in his mother's religious tradition, so Simone Weil was born into an atmosphere of 'Jewish agnosticism'. Thus, two potential sources of identity for Simone were minimized by her family: the family's Jewishness was scarcely acknowledged, and Simone Weil's gender was a topic that her parents studiously ignored or denigrated. Although Weil did not have a conventional religious background, and was not encouraged to be feminine in typical ways, still she was taught early the value of sacrifice. As an example, she related a story that she said had an influence on her entire life:

> The heroine of this fairy tale, who was sent by her stepmother into the forest, reaches a house where she is asked whether she wants to enter by the door in gold or the door in tar. 'For me', she replies, 'tar is quite good enough'. This was the right answer and a shower of gold fell on her. When her stepmother saw her bring back the

gold, she then sent her own daughter into the forest. But when asked the same question, her daughter chose the golden door and was deluged with tar. (in Pétrement, 1976, p. 9)

The mentality revealed by the heroine of this tale reflects the attitude of many Europeans of the early twentieth century. Self-sacrifice had become a way of life for Weil and her family as they approached World War I. Not only was Dr Weil an active member of the French army by the time the war began in 1914, but Simone was profoundly affected as well: at the age of only five, she stopped eating sugar and other foods that fighting soldiers did not have available to them. This sacrifice, like her earlier experiences with food, had long-term significance. She may have viewed this as a way of training herself to be equal to her brother, a child who, by the age of eight, had shown an amazing aptitude for mathematics, which his teachers viewed as an early sign of genius.

This effort notwithstanding, by the age of ten Simone Weil considered herself as lacking the natural abilities required of true genius, as she envisioned it – the ability to discern intellectual and moral 'truth' clearly and with relative ease. This early concern prefigures her later attitudes, including a statement made near the end of her life describing her childhood years:

> After months of inward darkness, I suddenly had the everlasting conviction that any human being, even though practically devoid of natural faculties, can penetrate to the kingdom of truth reserved for genius, if only he longs for truth and perpetually concentrates all his attention upon its attainment. (Weil, 1951a, p. 64)

Weil examines the nature of the concept of 'genius', assumed to be a 'natural' attribute by those people who labelled André Weil a 'mathematical genius' (Fiori, 1989, p. 19). In later years, she concludes that if genius is defined as having the capability of gaining insight into some fundamental universal truth, then the key to this capacity resides not so much in innate ability or aptitude (as in the case of her brother) as in sustained openness to insight, a form of concentration or *attente* (see Chapter 3 on attention). As Weil sees it, attention offers a form of genius available to anyone truly desirous of insight.

With such weighty thoughts on her mind, it is no surprise that by the age of twelve Weil had developed migraine headaches, which would continue to immobilize her for periods throughout her life. Her mother encouraged a spartan, naturalist attitude toward exercise and health, and in response to this her daughter often went without stockings even in extreme cold. Likewise, Selma Weil discouraged any stereotypical feminine behaviour. As she wrote in a letter to a friend, Mlle Chaintreuil, 'I am doing my best to encourage in Simone, not the graces of a little girl, but the straight-forwardness of a boy, even if she risks the appearance of rudeness' (Fiori, 1989, p. 24). In looking at the differences in how Selma Weil treated her children, readers may find it ironic that she puzzles over the contrast between her son's self-confidence and the fact that 'Simone, on the other hand, is always inclined to mistrust herself' (Pétrement, 1976, p. 3ff.).

Selma Weil insisted that her children be placed in lycée classes with the most highly respected teachers available and, in June 1925, Simone Weil earned a baccalauréat in philosophy. She entered Lycée Henry IV, where she encountered the philosopher, journalist and teacher, Emile-Auguste Chartier, known as Alain (1868–1952). His lectures and system of thought deeply influenced the formulation of Weil's own philosophy, and his comments on her writing and work indicate that he was equally impressed by her. He marked her work 'superior, and by a great margin to all the others of her generation' (Fiori, 1989, p. 37). In her first year at Lycée Henry IV, Weil began to associate with a group of young people who would act out plays and redress wrongs in imitation of the Knights of the Round Table. During this time, she began to wear a kind of medieval cape and sandals rather than shoes.

Later she also wore mannish suits and no hat, atypical dress for women of her time. As usual with Weil, what may seem to be peculiarities have a rational basis, and her dress code was no exception. These choices reflected more than mere eccentricity; they constituted a statement of the values that Weil maintained throughout her life: spirituality and egalitarianism in matters of economics and gender.

Despite Weil's academic success and her positive encounters with teachers like Alain, she often courted conflict with school officials who attempted to segregate the few females from the male majority. In her third year of study, Weil was even suspended for eight days for smoking in the men's courtyard; of course, all of the courtyards were for men. After gaining admittance in 1928 to the Ecole Normale Supérieure, the best school in France, she first encountered the syndicalist movement, La Révolution Prolétarienne. Her contact with this movement deepened her commitment to equality, and she demonstrated an affinity with a number of the causes of Marxism, trade unions and working-class and pacifist movements. During this time she also developed sinusitis, which weakened and debilitated her already fragile body. Despite her ill health, Weil completed her thesis, 'Science and perception in Descartes'. In July 1931 she passed her examinations, and in August she accepted her first teaching position: lecturer in philosophy at the girls' Lycée of Le Puy, where she met the well-known teacher and dedicated syndicalist, Urbain Thevenon. Becoming more and more fascinated with the life of common working people, she also attempted to immerse herself in the world of manual labour. In 1932 she hounded Guillot, a friend of Thevenon, to let her visit a coal mine, an extraordinary request from a woman, and it was granted. The experience of operating a compressed-air drill gave her such a headache that she almost fainted, and, although she requested a job in the mine, Thevenon explained to her that this would not be possible.

In another effort at firsthand experience, Weil visited Germany in 1932 and stayed with a worker's family, 'to attempt to understand what the force of Fascism rested on' (Fiori, 1989, p. 73). She published an essay about this experience, 'L'Allemagne en attente', which was printed in the pamphlet, *La Révolution prolétarienne* (Fiori, 1989, p. 73). International Communist activists were outraged by Weil's description of the inaction of German Communist Party members. This and similar experiences gave her the basis for some of her most profound and original social-political commentary, in which she melds concrete experience with a theoretical framework. Her commitment to the workers' cause inspired her to support demonstrations, an activity which eventually resulted in her being transferred to another teaching post at Roanne in 1933. She continued to support labour movements and, later, to search relentlessly for spiritual truth, all the while gaining a reputation for being a communist and an atheist. The latter accusation takes on enormous irony when considered in light of her later writings and actions, as does the former in light of her statement that 'it is not religion but revolution which is the opium of the people' (Weil, 1963, p. xxvii).

In 1934, she took a job as a factory hand at the Société de Constructions Electriques et Mécaniques Alsthom in Paris, where she later worked as a packer. Weil was determined to follow her doctrine of the popularization of knowledge, and she strived to achieve this goal both by educating herself about the lives of the people she wished to serve and by serving the people with whom she worked. During her year at the factory, from 1934 to 1935, Weil underwent an amazing yet subtle transformation – a metamorphosis that preserved themes from her early life, while altering the primary intellectual frame of reference from which she addressed lifelong philosophical dilemmas. Specifically, her writing assumed a decidedly spiritual direction, one that can be seen as simultaneously more abstract *and* more practical. In her journals, she explores in great detail the actual mechanisms of oppression and the relationship between material circumstances and spiritual or intellectual behaviour. During this period she also had 'contacts with Catholicism that really counted' (Pétrement, 1976, pp. 215–16), although initially there was no discernible change in her outward behaviour. At the same time, Weil began to talk of dying, and she attended to her own health so little that her friends and family feared she might indeed work herself to death.

In Bourges, between 1935 and 1936, Weil tried unsuccessfully to obtain work at the Rosière Foundries. She talked to workers at the Rosière plant about their working conditions, even after she returned to teaching philosophy. During this time she suffered from constant headaches, and she considered taking time off to recuperate physically, in order to be better able to write and work. However, she then opted for a different alternative and wrote to a friend: 'Or rather this is the way out: keep on pushing myself as long as it will be possible for me – and when the disproportion between the tasks that have to be accomplished and my ability to work will have become too great, then die' (Pétrement, 1976, p. 261).

From 1936 to 1937 Weil responded to the Spanish Civil War, first by trying to help prevent war, and then by attempting to share in the struggle and suffering of those on the front lines. Her parents followed her to Spain only to discover that, either in her nearsightedness or clumsiness, she had walked into or spilled a pot of boiling oil and had suffered a severe burn. Her injury kept her from facing the dilemma with which she had wrestled intensely – whether to remain passive or to try to kill the enemy and, in the process, risk killing an innocent victim. Later on, a visit to Italy allowed her further escape from politics in a renewed passion for beauty in literature and art. She was nevertheless disheartened to find among workers in Italy the same dispirited resignation she had recognized in her fellow French workers.

Upon returning to France in 1937, Weil obtained a teaching post at Saint-Quentin. Headaches continued to plague her, and in 1938 she asked for sick leave from her teaching assignments. During this year, a young Englishman introduced her to the English metaphysical poets of the seventeenth century, and she later commented that George Herbert's poem 'Love' had influenced and moved her deeply, something we discuss later in relation to Weil's mysticism. When in 1940 the Vichy anti-Jewish laws required her dismissal from teaching, she experienced this removal as a devastating blow. The following year, however, she met the Reverend Father J. M. Perrin at a Dominican monastery in Marseilles, and he helped her find farm work through his friend, Gustave Thibon. While working in the vineyards, Weil continued to learn about the dehumanizing elements of manual labour, which were exaggerated by her own lack of manual dexterity. She also persisted in trying to bring intellectual discussions into the world of labourers. At the same time, she carried on lively theological discussions and debates with Father Perrin and Thibon, and her thinking and writing took an even more distinctly religious turn, one wherein she even considered the merits of baptism into the Catholic Church.

Arriving in the United States in 1942, Weil contacted Simone Dietz, whom she had first met in Marseilles and with whom she hoped to travel to England to join the war effort. To prepare for this mission, the two went so far as to take a first aid course in Harlem, where they were the only white women in the class (in Pétrement, 1976, p. 477). Also during this time, Weil began attending mass daily, while continuing her efforts to reach England and participate in the French Resistance movement. Eventually, she contacted Maurice Schumann (who had been a schoolmate and pupil of Alain at the Ecole Normale, a fellow French Resistance member and lifelong friend, and who in time would become De Gaulle's foreign minister) to obtain information about travelling to London. With his assistance, Weil was able to make it as far as Liverpool, where she was placed in a wartime detention camp because of her subversive status as a presumed communist. She later gained release only with Schumann's help.

As she had done as a child during the previous war, Weil again refused to eat because she wanted to share in the suffering and deprivation of soldiers and citizens in German-occupied France. She was working at the Ministry of the Interior for the Commissariat of Action for France, and in this capacity she was assigned by the Free French organization in London to produce reports related to the postwar reconstruction of France. These writings resulted in the main political work of her later years, *The Need for Roots*, published posthumously in 1949 (English translation 1952). In April 1943 she collapsed and was diagnosed with tuberculosis, a condition the doctors initially felt could be cured with rest and a hearty diet, but these were luxuries Weil resolutely denied herself until she had little choice in the matter. Her illness isolated her from the few acquaintances she had in England, and her refusal or inability to eat annoyed some of the physicians and nurses who were caring for her, especially when it became apparent that she was not going to recover. However, a handful of French friends and acquaintances visited her until her death.

During the final days of her life, her letters tell a poignant story – especially when contrasted with the reality of her existence. It is clear that Weil both anticipates her own death and is enormously frustrated and discouraged by her inability to join directly with her compatriots in their struggle against Fascism. At the same time, she maintains a resolute cheerfulness and breezy tone in most of her communications with her family. In July 1943, for instance, she wrote to her mother, still keeping from her parents the severity of her physical condition, a secretiveness that must have been torture considering her reverence for her parents (Weil, 1965, p. 257). This last letter to her parents exemplifies her concern for their well-being and her desire to shield them from worry:

I have little time or inspiration for letters now. They will be short, rare and infrequent. But you have another major source of comfort. . . . When you have received this letter (unless it is especially fast) you will already have received the expected cable. (Nothing for certain! . . .) Good bye, darlings. Thousands and thousands of caresses.
 Simone

(Weil, 1965, p. 253)

Despite Weil's apparently unreserved regard and consideration for her parents, it might be an error to interpret her devotion at face value. She was, after all, the younger sister of a son who had first place in the family: as the firstborn, in receiving attention not usually given to a second child; as a son, in receiving privileged treatment from a mother who avowedly despised the gender roles normally assigned to girls; and as a supposed genius, in being expected to succeed. For Simone Weil, self-starvation may have been a means of establishing identity and independence within this family structure.

Weil's death had come to seem inevitable to her and to those around her. On 17 August 1943, Simone Weil was admitted to Grosvenor Sanatorium in Ashford, Kent, as close to her beloved France as possible. She refused food, as she had been doing for some time, grew steadily weaker, and died on Tuesday, 24 August, at the age of thirty-four. She was buried in Grave No. 79, Ashford New Cemetery, with only seven people in attendance at her funeral. Simone Weil's landlady, Mrs Francis, and her old friend Maurice Schumann were there, along with her friends Mrs Rosin, Thérèse Closon, Suzanne Aron (a lycée friend and wife of the sociologist and politician Raymond Aron), and Professor Fehling (with whom she had vacationed long ago in Montana). Because the Catholic priest who had agreed to come did not arrive, Schumann read the prayers, while the landlady, Mrs Francis, placed a bunch of flowers tied with the red, white and blue of France on the coffin. Simone Weil was buried as a pauper, a classification which meant that no marker except a number was placed on the grave. Weil's parents learned of her death only after the burial had taken place.

Some newspapers published articles with headlines such as FRENCH PROFESSOR STARVES HERSELF TO DEATH and DEATH FROM STARVATION: FRENCH PROFESSOR'S CURIOUS SACRIFICE (Pétrement, 1976, p. 537). For some time Weil's grave was unmarked except for grass and a plot number, and few people even knew of her death. As the years passed, however, more and more people made pilgrimages to her graveside, and a group of distinguished authors purchased a simple stone to mark her birth and death. Today, most people in Ashford are aware of the famous French philosopher buried under towering trees in their new cemetery. Nevertheless, her brilliance remains under a cloud of obscurity, and for a philosopher and thinker of her exceptional gifts, she is still relatively little known or understood outside select academic circles.

On not being an insider

Simone Weil's position as an outsider has been greatly emphasized. Thus positioned, Weil stands out as being different from representatives of various factions, movements and subcultural groups with whom she might have aligned. Rather than connect to social groups by strategic identification, she excelled at pointing out flaws, shortcomings and half-truths embedded in organizations and philosophies of her time. However, simply to categorize Weil as an outsider obscures an understanding of her intentions. It is perhaps more accurate to say that Simone Weil intentionally chose never to be an insider – regardless of the intrinsic merits of a given group – because she mistrusted the perspective of the insider.

Weil understood that to reside inside a group necessarily distances one from those outside it. Her favourite teacher at the lycée, Alain, called her 'The Martian', to indicate 'that she had nothing in common with us and was sovereignly judging us all' (Pétrement, 1976, p. 65). Eric Springsted argues that 'paradoxically, it is because she was an outsider, and still remains one, that she has so much to offer to those of us who are not' (Springsted, 1986, p. 7). In what ways did she defy convention? Gabriella Fiori describes Weil's 'awkward and strange displays of her being exceptional', including sleeping on the floor and wearing sackcloth and sandals or, on occasion, bare feet (Fiori, 1989, pp. 304–5). Simone de Beauvoir admired her, but was rebuffed by Weil as someone who had 'never gone hungry' (De Beauvoir, 1958, pp. 236–7). Robert Coles notes that Weil was 'forever on the move, morally and spiritually and politically and culturally, so that, by the time Hitler forced her and her family into exile, she was already chronically displaced' (Coles, 1987, p. 5). Some of Weil's sense of displacement was certainly imposed upon her, but much of it was a deliberate ethical choice. Having been a victim of gender and ethnic stereotyping as a woman entering intellectual communities and as a woman and intellectual entering worker communities, Weil was determined not to cut others off in similar fashion. Intentionally violating expectations and rejecting labels for herself, she also refused to categorize and pre-judge others according to social group.

A more accurate description of Simone Weil's placement in the surrounding culture is that she was at the intersection of a number of groups. In her writings, Weil is explicitly interested in the interstices, the boundaries between categories – a fascination that seemed to define her social and spiritual situation and even to affect her perceptions of her own physical condition. For example, she described a headache that she claimed 'never stopped for a second' from 1930 to 1940, resulting in pain she felt at the 'central point of the nervous system . . . the meeting place of soul and body' (Rees, 1966, p. 15). Clearly this was no ordinary headache. It seemed to signify for her a necessary pain or tension imposed by the disparity between physical and psychic realms – an agonizing pull on her consciousness from opposing categories of existence. Her commitment to remaining on the boundaries of social and spiritual domains is reflected in her discussion of her attitude towards the important categories of class, race, and religion:

> It is the sign of a vocation, the vocation to remain in a sense anonymous, ever ready to be mixed into the paste of common humanity. . . . I have the essential need, and I think I can say the vocation, to move among men of every class and complexion, mixing with them and sharing their life and outlook, so far that is to say as conscience allows, merging into the crowd and disappearing among them, so that they show themselves as they are, putting off all disguises with me. It is because I long to know them so as to love them just as they are. For if I do not love them as they are, it will not be they whom I love, and my love will be unreal. (Weil, 1951a, pp. 48–9)

She expresses a similar desire in the spiritual domain as she does in the social realm, a commitment which prevented her from ever formally converting to Catholicism:

> Having so intense and so painful a sense of this urgency [of the need for a truly Incarnated Christianity], I should betray the truth, that is to say the aspect of the truth that I see, if I left the point, where I have been since my birth, at the intersection of Christianity and everything that is not Christianity.
>
> I have always remained at this exact point, on the threshold of the Church, without moving, quite still, ἐν ὑπομένη [in endurance]. (Weil, 1951a, pp. 75–6)

Because Weil sought depersonalization as a pathway to truth, she resisted identification with any particular group. J. P. Little suspects that 'may help to explain in part her attitude towards her Jewishness and her femininity, both aspects of herself which were less than universal, demanding specific responses and specific patterns of behaviour to which she was not prepared to conform' (Little, 1988, pp. 156–7). Weil was egalitarian in her rejection of group identification. As the daughter of secular Jews, she did not generally associate with Jewish religious or cultural communities, and some of her criticisms of the Hebrew tradition have prompted critics to label her 'anti-Semitic'. Her allegiance to her gender label was similarly negligible, if it existed at all; when asked once to speak on the subject of feminism, she refused, stating that she was not a feminist. Ironically, it is likely that one of the directions Weil might have taken had she lived longer would have been toward a more consciously feminist stance. She participated in a number of activities not usually considered appropriate for women, in part due to her fierce belief in the principles of equality. In the field of politics, her alliance with socialist groups and causes did not prevent her from getting into a vociferous dispute with Leon Trotsky when she finally had the opportunity to meet him in December 1933 (Pétrement, 1976, p. 47). In her later years, despite her admiration for Catholicism and her close friendships with priests and religious figures, she never would 'betray the truth' by joining the Catholic Church. Clearly, Simone Weil charted her own course.

Because many of her contemporaries did not appreciate the subtleties of Weil's ideas and modes of expression, she did not appear enlightened to some of the important thinkers and leaders of her time. Indeed, she struck a number of people as odd. And considered within the context of certain endeavours that she attempted, she can even be seen as downright ludicrous or pathetic, most particularly in her attempts to be a factory worker, an occupation for which she could not have been more ill suited. Yet this same activity may be interpreted in terms of her belief that only through doing could one know the subject. When interpreted in the light of this belief, the action crystallizes as a meaningful attempt to know at first hand the conditions endured by most workers. For Weil, the connection between truth, love and human experience was crucial:

> To desire truth is to desire direct contact with a piece of reality. To desire contact with a piece of reality is to love. We desire truth only in order to love in truth. We desire to know the truth about what we love. Instead of talking about love of truth, it would be better to talk about the spirit of truth in love. (Weil, 1952, p. 253)

This search for truth coloured all of her activities, and while she derived satisfaction from producing actual goods, she gained much more than this. She achieved an unprecedented intimate insight into concepts of labour and production that she chose to analyse and explore in her writing.

In spite of scholarly attention that has focused on her idiosyncrasies, it would be a mistake to conclude that Simone Weil's life was a failure. A number of themes in her life and work resonate with her generation and subsequent generations who have found themselves in moral dilemmas. Far from being a 'voice crying in the wilderness', as some commentators have described her (Coles, 1987, p. 30), she was a voice speaking for her age. World political events may have prevented Weil's words from reaching her contemporaries before her death, but her thoughts and writings have proved increasingly influential for generations coming to maturity after World War II. Knowledge of her work and the influence of her ideas has increased steadily, and of course the publication of this book is demonstration that a new audience has been reached.

Weil's thought mirrored the growing concerns and beliefs of her time and ours; however, her idiosyncrasies and atypical behaviours are for some the major source of fascination. For many of her biographers, the most outstanding single feature of her personal life was the apparent self-starvation, which resulted in her death from tuberculosis (although one can argue that this disease alone could eventually have killed her). Most commentators use the term anorexia to refer to her behaviour, but a more fruitful line of inquiry would be to explore the phenomenon of self-starvation as it relates to broader life themes and to larger segments of society, including women, political protesters, religious figures and others who choose not to eat. Was Simone Weil's refusal to eat a symbolic, heroic act, or was it simply a manifestation of pathology? Anna Freud in particular has disagreed with the latter conclusion. In an interview with Robert Coles, Freud pointed out distinctions between Weil's refusal to eat and the typical pattern of anorexia nervosa. She concluded that 'Simone Weil doesn't seem to have had any delusions of obesity, or at least, hasn't described her fatness as the enemy. . . . She was articulate, and she was determined, and if she was also sick – in her head first, and later, her body – then we'd better be careful about how we refer to that sickness' (in Coles, 1987, pp. 27–8). Weil's aversion to food is not interwoven with distorted self-perceptions of her physical body, nor is she concerned at all about 'being overweight' or 'feeling fat'. On the contrary, her refusals to eat always seem to reflect a social or spiritual concern rather than a sense of physical inadequacy. Had Weil's refusals been performed by a male, it is unlikely they would have been labelled anorexic at all. No one talks of Mahatma Gandhi, for instance, as an anorexic. In fact, even identifying the phenomenon of anorexia as an 'eating disorder' more noteworthy than, say, coronary-prone patterns of over-eating demonstrates a difference of valuation by gender. As Matra Robertson observes,

> [W]hile self-starvation is certainly life-threatening, mortality statistics indicate that heart disease is the major cause of death in New South Wales. How is it that men with beer bellies, as they court death (according to the medical literature) by excessive drinking and eating, are not also generally referred to psychiatrists? The dominant discourses regarding the body position men and women in different places. (Robertson, 1992, p. 17)

A similar problem pertaining to gender informs many physical descriptions of Weil by biographers, even if they did not believe she was anorexic. For example, Pétrement describes her as making herself unattractive (Pétrement, 1976, p. 26), while Rees remarks that 'a plain neatness was the most she even aimed at in her appearance' (Rees, 1966, p. 10). Michele Murray describes 'her ugliness – for by now the beautiful child had become an ugly woman who dressed in ill-fitting clothes and spoke strangely, peering at the world from behind thick glasses, constantly smoking, her fingers stained with nicotine, her rasping cough a regular accompaniment to her monologues – and she was unlikely to appeal to anyone lacking her gifts and her obsessions' (Murray, 1973, p. 213). Considered in context, Weil's refusal to follow dress codes defined by gender and class was consistent with her rejection of a consumer culture and her ethical commitment to equality and selflessness; in other words, her pattern of dress may be seen as consistent with her pattern of eating.

While the intensity of Weil's rejection of convention may be unique, changes in dress and behaviour were actually common among idealistic members of the intelligentsia in post-World War I Europe. During World War II, self-sacrifice and devaluing of conspicuous consumption spread into the rest of the population as well, and it became patriotic to sacrifice for the war effort. Many people made dietary sacrifices, because it seemed somehow appropriate in the face of news about massive deprivation and suffering. Simone Weil's willingness to forgo 'luxuries' of clothing and food during this period may be unusual primarily in the degree to which she practised self-denial.

The perennial debate over whether Simone Weil's final act of self-starvation was pathological may perhaps be resolved by this attention to context. For Weil, living between world wars, the act of physical nourishment became wedded to her quest for artistic, economic, political and spiritual truth. Her own refusal to eat reflected a sense of connection with all of humanity, a theme intentionally constructed as counter to consuming goods, because consumption inevitably implies competition for resources. Ellmann observes that such a mode of expression may be easily misconstrued, given the *Zeitgeist* of twentieth-century civilization: 'The image of the starving artist . . . seems to stand . . . for the exclusion of artists from the life of commerce and their proud refusal to be "fed" by capital' (Ellmann, 1993, p. 70). In a capitalist society, however, people see happiness as tied inextricably to consuming, not to being consumed by or sacrificing themselves to some higher purpose. The dominant motif of capitalism involves patterns of thought and habits of behaviour that emphasize the acquiring and consuming of goods ('eating'). Within such a context, is it any wonder that Simone Weil initially appears so incomprehensible?

Weil also failed to be appreciated by the academic community of her time, and neglect by academics continues to this day. Mary Dietz notes:

> [A]lthough Weil's writings have been admired and cited by a generation of thinkers and writers as diverse as Albert Camus, Martin Buber, T. S. Eliot, Dwight MacDonald, Hannah Arendt, and Czeslaw Milosz, they have been largely ignored by the academic community. Her life has been chronicled in numerous biographies and biographical essays, but her thought has not been subjected to the same detailed exploration that distinguishes many of her contemporaries – Jean-Paul Sartre, for example, or Raymond Aron, Albert Camus, Hannah Arendt, Gertrude Stein, Simone de Beauvoir, and George Orwell – the latter of whom has often inspired comparison with Weil. (Dietz, 1987, p. xiii)

What kind of thinker is she?

Weil's emphasis on the integration of apparently contradictory elements is an important characteristic of her approach. While she proposes links between such apparently disparate activities as factory work and meditation, this linkage is not a random or haphazard muddling of categories of thought. Weil advocated a relentless struggle for truth. She could also see value in a process, even if it is fraught with error:

So it comes about that, paradoxical as it may seem, a Latin prose or a geometry problem, even though done wrong, may be of great service one day provided we devote the right kind of effort to them. Should the occasion arise, they can one day make us better able to give someone . . . exactly the help required to save him. (Weil, 1951a, p. 75–6)

The metaphor of nourishment, found throughout her work, highlights what it is that makes Weil simultaneously appealing and distressing for many feminists of her own age and of the current period. Much that is noble and generous in Weil reflects selflessness and appreciation of others, twin characteristics considered an extension of the traditionally feminine values of nurturing, compassion and self-sacrifice. At the same time that Sybil Oldfield among others applauds Weil's rejection of masculine principles of domination and force (Oldfield, 1989, p. 74), other feminist thinkers are uncomfortable with the stereotypical aspects of the martyred female – an image and role model that many women have imitated throughout the centuries.

Weil died the year before women were granted the vote in France. According to Simone Pétrement, both Weil and her parents wished that she had been born a male, something Pétrement interprets as a family joke with serious consequences. She notes that 'her parents called her "Simon," "our son number two," and "our cagne boy,"' and Simone later signed her letters Simon. If it looks at first as if Pétrement is about to interpret the subtext of this 'game', she quickly explains it away with the same reasons that Weil herself would probably have assigned; that is, the tasks she is destined to undertake 'demand of her masculine qualities and strengths' (Pétrement, 1976, p. 27). Pétrement does not tackle the psychological ramifications of having a lifelong belief that one has been born with the wrong gender, nor does Weil explore the issue in a serious manner, even in her personal journals.

Of all the metaphors and symbols Weil uses to express spiritual truths, images pertaining to food and nourishment cross boundaries of time and space; we find them across a variety of subject matters and through varied periods of her life. Indeed, the image of 'eating' and her precept of *attente* (attention) comprise the central metaphors of her life. Both concepts reflect a larger cultural concern. As Matra Robertson notes in *Starving in the Silences*, 'In Western society, food signifies success and failure; temptation and restraint; force and freedom' (Robertson, 1992, p. 72). The key here is that Weil seems to view restraint as a key to contact with the divine. Like Kierkegaard's God, the God of Simone Weil is hidden and distant. Although Weil has philosophical and logical reasons for seeing creation as a manifestation of 'other-than-God', the psychological reasons for her perceptions may be useful as well in demonstrating how women have come to view themselves in relation to knowledge and even in relation to their own bodies.

Weil's work is steeped in analysis of what current feminists would identify as a patriarchal philosophical tradition. While some feminists argue for a position outside the dualist, binary logic of phallocentric psychology and philosophy, Irigaray counters that 'we do not escape so easily from reversal. We do not escape in particular by thinking we can dispense with a rigorous interpretation of phallocentrism. This is no simple manageable way to leap to the outside' (Irigaray, 1985, p. 162). Simone Weil constantly sought ways to 'leap to the outside', despite the rigorous training she received in traditional scholarly modes. Weil's thought often embraces binary oppositions and the terms of patriarchal philosophy and reason, only to transcend and reconfigure the discussion on a spiritual plane. This kind of reconfiguring and rereading places Weil among the few who manage at times to step outside the confines of cultural dictates.

As acute as Weil's insights are into the nature of other individuals and social entities, she seems incapable of this kind of understanding about her own personal condition. Indeed, she seemed to view her own body as an impediment rather than a source of fulfilment. She accepted the model of restraint as virtue, even though she had different (and more complex) reasons for this acceptance than the simple-minded dualism that pervades much of Western thought, that spirituality is good and physicality is evil. Weil recognized how the enslavement of workers convinces them of their own inadequacy, but she failed to make such a connection between her own self-concept and self-sacrificing (even self-punishing) behaviour. Of all the groups from which Simone Weil distanced herself, the two that seem most formative of her identity – women and Jews – were the two from which she seemed most alienated. At the same time, her decision not to see herself as only Jewish or only female distinguishes one of the most admirable aspects of Weil's thought – her refusal to accept the designation of Other, so often placed on such groups by the larger society. It is crucial to recognize this tension in order to understand much of what Simone Weil has to say.

Weil felt little allegiance to the academic world. Her method of teaching was unconventional and interdisciplinary, often ignoring the rote memorization that ensured passing the baccalauréat. Mark Taylor observes, 'It is worth noting that an inordinately high percentage of her own lycée students failed their baccalauréat exams, a fact that bothered her not a bit' (Taylor, 1973, p. 450). Later, Weil chose to take time off from teaching to work in the Renault plant, and she eventually lost her job as a lycée instructor in 1941 when the new laws against Jews forced her resignation from the state education service. Instead of seeking similar employment as a tutor, she opted again for manual labour. After 1941, however, Weil continued to write and engage in philosophical and intellectual inquiry. Early in her life, she remarked that she longed to have the insight afforded to her older brother, and at age fourteen she 'felt it better to die than to live without truth' (in Rees, 1966, p. 13). Eventually she decided 'that any human being at all, even if his natural faculties are almost nil, finds his way into that realm of truth which is reserved for genius, if only he longs for truth and makes a perpetual effort of attention so as to reach it' (ibid., p. 14). Her brother described her vocation as that of 'saint', and certainly a number of her actions and attitudes place her in the company of people who have that title; indeed, one of her nurses called her a saint when Weil was only eight years old (Cameron, 1981, p. 36). T. S. Eliot, in his introduction to *The Need for Roots*, discusses her saintly characteristics in the following terms:

> Simone Weil was one who might have become a saint. Like some who have achieved this state, she had greater obstacles to overcome, as well as greater strength for overcoming them, than the rest of us. A potential saint can be a very difficult person: I suspect that Simone Weil could be at times insupportable. One is struck, here and there, by a contrast between an almost superhuman humility and what appears to be an almost outrageous arrogance. (Eliot, in Weil, 1952, p. vi)

Whether one applies the label of 'saint' or 'heretic', however, Weil is not so easily categorized. She possessed the kind of mind that defied categorization, for she was always seeking to find a vision outside the mainstream, to find the most idiosyncratic understanding of what others took for granted as truth. The unusualness which marks her analysis also made her prey to extreme pronouncements on her ideas and personality. Leslie Fiedler calls her a 'tragic buffoon' (Fiedler, 1951, p. 38), while Martin Buber refers to her 'far-reaching negation of life' (Buber, 1952, p. 33). Despite some of the initial harsh judgements she has received, she has proven to be, as Arnold describes her, 'one of those lonely figures belonging to no party, yet claimed by all' (Arnold, 1951, p. 3). In recent years this has become even more true. Her tendency to make problematic what others consider 'normal' anticipates trends in criticism and scholarship by some forty years. Weil was indeed different in some fundamental way from each of the groups with whom she found affinities. But perhaps her differences lie not so much in quality or kind as in degree.

Although Weil's thought and activities aroused some interest among a small circle of intellectuals while she was still alive, her works were not published in her lifetime. Aside from *The Need for Roots* (1952), most of her works have been compiled from notebooks, essays, and scraps of thought hastily jotted down. This organization was itself a challenge, and English translations came later and quite haphazardly. Despite scholarly frustration over this style of collection, the amorphous quality of the writings is actually in keeping with Weil's sense of propriety. Consequently, Weil's work may best be approached by sampling or dipping into it at various points, much as one now reads post-modern texts, or even computer hypertexts (which provide easy transport from one topic to another, by simply clicking on any bold-faced word in the text). Certainly, it is possible to group Weil's writings in order to facilitate understanding, but such organization should not violate Weil's intent to show connections and relationships among supposedly discrete entities.

Despite her commitment to crossing boundaries, the vast majority of secondary works on Weil treat her life and thought from a theological perspective rather than a political or philosophical one, even though she wrote at least as much about the latter as she did about religion. Because her religious works were published first, however, and because of a general failure in her readership to understand mystical experience, she was identified early as a difficult, 'obscure' mystic, rather than as a flesh and blood woman dedicated to achieving authentic readings of reality in all important life arenas. This tendency towards a theological perspective on her life and work has constituted a major barrier to Weil's wider influence. Few people become interested in Weil without having a strong interest in Christian, Catholic or mystical religious experience, and the vast majority of those who write about Weil are religious. Thus, her religious statements can easily be cited as a further proof of the legitimacy of commentators' own beliefs, while the rest of her work is downplayed or ignored. On the other hand, those scholars who assume explicitly psychological or philosophical perspectives can just as easily ignore 'inconvenient' aspects of her work. In either case, it is essential to consider that what *draws* a reader to Weil's work may be precisely the element that *obscures* a view of the whole person and prevents exploration of the full range of her thinking.

Most contemporaneous accounts of Weil's life came from friends and relatives, and the earliest subsequent biographies compare Weil with notable figures in order to assess her work and life. These attempts to place her work in context consistently aimed at locating her within patriarchal psychological, religious or philosophical frameworks. Thus in Coles's biography, *Simone Weil: A Modern Pilgrimage* (1987), Anna Freud attempts to analyse whether or not Weil fits the pattern of anorexia or some other disorder. As an author concerned with Catholicism, Coles himself discusses Weil's work in relation to Flannery O'Connor, who was also a writer and a devout Catholic, as if this comparison might yield some special insight into her religious and literary thinking. In *The Wine of Absurdity* (1966) Paul West includes analysis of the work of Simone Weil compared with that of T. S. Eliot and Graham Greene, again with an eye to placing her within a religious tradition. Concerned with broader existentialist issues, John M. Dunaway's discussion of 'Estrangement and the need for roots' argues for the possible influence of Simone Weil on the writing of Albert Camus, who called her the 'only great mind' of their time. Even if this is an exaggeration on Camus and Dunaway's part, it is accurate to say that 'Camus and Weil brought to bear on the crisis of culture in the twentieth century two prophetic voices schooled among the same tutors and full of the same profound compassion for a world exiled from the kingdom of rootedness' (Dunaway, 1985, p. 42). This attention to the concept of roots makes such analysis more universal than some others, since it may apply to a variety of philosophical stances.

Another major category of response to Weil's work combines aesthetic and emotional identification with the example of her life, primarily from a feminist perspective. As a tribute to the extent of her own identification with Weil, Megan Terry wrote the play *Approaching Simone*, performed at La Mama theatre in New York and published by The Feminist Press in 1973. An introduction by Phyllis Jane Wagner provides analysis and commentary on Terry's motivation for writing the work, and it places both Weil and Terry within the context of feminist thought. In a similarly autobiographical approach, Weil also appears in a feminist anthology entitled *Between Women* (Ascher et al., 1993). In this work, Michele Cliff describes her early encounters with the work of Weil in 'Sister/outsider: some thoughts on Simone Weil', a meditation on the influence of Weil on Cliff's development as a woman and an artist. Another homage to the pain and courage of Weil appears in poetic form, as Stephanie Strickland describes the life and thought of Weil in *The Red Virgin: A Poem of Simone Weil* (1993).

In contrast to these more aesthetic and affective responses, Sybil Oldfield places Weil in the context of women's resistance to militarism during the years of 1900 to 1989 in *Women against the Iron Fist* (1989). Although Oldfield's work is less emotional and more historical, she shares with the previous works a highly personal response to Weil. It is also clear that, regardless of the genre or approach, many of these authors view her as an early feminist model, worthy not merely of sympathy but of emulation. In *Women against the Iron Fist* Sybil Oldfield describes Weil in touching, even intimate tones, indicating the hope and inspiration her writings and personal life have provided:

> [H]aunted by the hunger of those fallen into Nazi hands, Simone Weil either could not, or would not, eat. 'The suffering all over the world obsesses and overwhelms me to the point of annihilating my faculties,' she wrote to Maurice Schumann at the end of July 1942. On 24 August 1943, aged thirty-four, she died. (Oldfield, 1989, p. 95)

Oldfield describes the shock of Alain, Weil's former teacher, who was so moved by Weil's example as to offer her these final words: 'When she went into politics I expected much. Much? I expected, quite simply, the answer' (ibid.).

Situating Simone Weil

As well as providing a general assessment of her ideas and writings, it is also important to assess Simone Weil's place within a genealogy of 'women of ideas'. We are considerably persuaded by Andrea Nye's (1994) approach, which refuses any simple distinction between those women of ideas who were feminist and those who were not. Instead, Nye is concerned with recovering an alternative tradition of women's thought, one in which

> it may be possible to trace other lines of thought, not protests against male bias, not the passionate complaints of victims of injustice, but a continuing meditation by women on the human condition that develops positive concepts, arguments, and ways of knowing to inform women's, and men's, ways in the world. In order to recover such a line of thought it may be necessary to abandon the requirement that texts of interest to feminists must deal primarily with gender. It may be necessary to give up the hope that if sexism can somehow be eliminated there will be no more conflict. . . . But the conflicts were not invented by men. They are an effect of the human condition, female and male: we are physical and moral creatures; painful labour is necessary for survival; human nature is individual and social; physical causation rules the natural world at the same time as there are values that transcend material life. At these radical points of contradiction women's thought might be valuable. (Nye, 1994, p. xvi)

Nye herself is concerned with offering broad overviews of the thinking on such fundamental features of the human condition provided by Rosa Luxemburg, Hannah Arendt – and also Simone Weil. As Nye points out, none of these three women thinkers theorized Fascism or capitalism as patriarchal (sexism was a dimension of oppression they hardly discussed), they used suspect 'generic' language, and they were immersed in no supportive networks of women scholars. However, these things provided strengths, as well as weaknesses, within their work, because by '[b]ypassing the very real fact of women's oppression, they took upon themselves the authority to rethink the human condition' (Nye, 1994, p. xviii). And 'the human condition' in its broadest sense is of course of crucial concern within feminist thinking, and certainly within any attempt to construct the genealogy of women of ideas.

This genealogy is composed in part by those women thinkers who define their ideas and work in opposition or resistance to the male tradition, an approach adopted by most if not all feminist work. But it is surely also composed by those women who as it were have bypassed the 'malestream' of canonical thought, ideas and intellectual, political and moral positions. It is our conviction that Simone Weil is a central thinker from this branch of the genealogy of women of ideas.

Perhaps the leitmotif of Weil's thought and work is her refusal to accept the conventional academic disjuncture between thought and action; for her, thought is justified by its application, its use in the world. Accordingly, she advocated a 'proper relationship' between thought and action. For instance, Weil applied her attention (a central concept in her thinking) to suffering, the suffering that came about because of force resulting from war and oppression certainly, but also that which arose from the more mundane and everyday workings of power. Attending to oppression, force and suffering means being alive to the complexities of their interrelation as well as their origin, and such complexities mean that 'reality' is also deeply contradictory. Thus, while the mainstream of Western thought may be concerned with consistency, in considerable contrast Simone Weil, long before postmodernist and deconstructionist ideas became current, was concerned with recognizing the absence of consistency in life, the continual presence of reversals and contradictions, and the unavoidable existence of these even within 'solutions' to problems of the human condition. She argued that contradictory truths coexist, and that such contradictions must be used 'like pincers' to grasp the truth beyond.

Weil's identification with the oppressed began in her early childhood and continued throughout her life. It is a theme that may well be a mainspring of much of her thinking and action, as well as a theme that attracts many of her readers. However, it also constitutes the element of her work – and her life – that readers find most difficult to come to terms with. Aligning herself with the most wretched, those who suffered most, Weil lived in circumstances of privation, particularly where food was concerned. For her it was not enough to condemn, for example, poverty and the results of war; these experiences had to be directly entered into and lived before a social theorist could truly understand them. That is, for Simone Weil working through complexities and contradictions cannot be done by effort of will and intellect alone, however important these may be. The key is attention, the insistence on facing unpalatable truths and contradictions and the acceptance of uncertainties; but for Weil this must be combined with entering into the experience of oppression and suffering as closely as possible, even if doing so took her beyond the limits of what was considered 'normal' or 'acceptable' – and even if it meant endangering herself or bringing about her injury or death.

These central elements of Simone Weil's thought led her to think and to write, and to act, on a wide range of topics and issues. As the chapters that follow will show, her work, most of it unpublished in her lifetime, thoughtfully engages crucial aspects of the human condition, including politics and labour, science and knowledge, education and apprenticeship schemes, nationalism and Fascism, evil and good, and much more. While Weil did not identify herself as a feminist, nor theorize patriarchy or sexism, nevertheless in the genealogy of women of ideas she is powerfully and insightfully present as someone who most certainly, in Nye's words, 'took upon herself the authority to rethink the human condition'.

Science and Knowledge
The Perceiving Self

In this chapter and those that follow, we present Simone Weil's work on its own terms – to allow Weil to communicate her vision by speaking in her own voice, in selected excerpts from her writings. The metaphors of vision and voice are apt, because much of her work concerns the need to examine reality carefully and to refine rigorously all perceptual readings. Even Weil's choice of dissertation topic, 'Science and perception in Descartes', reflects her search for the clearest possible understanding of the universe and her search for a method capable of providing such a rendering.

In an important discussion of Weil's contribution to philosophical thought, Dorothy Tuck McFarland argues that Weil traces her unification of science and metaphysics to Descartes, 'who is usually considered responsible for the unbridgeable gulf between them. In this early essay, she argues plainly . . . for an end to the tyranny of savants and specialists of all kinds; more broadly, she is looking for a philosophical base that will not support any form of authoritarianism, and a philosophy of reflection that emphasizes the individual thinker as knower'

(McFarland, 1983, p. 28). McFarland's recognition is an important one, not least because it helps to distinguish Weil's Cartesian influences from those elements of Descartes that influenced the development of positivism. In introducing some of Weil's lesser-known essays, McFarland states that the 'coup that she attempted to bring off in her thesis was a proof of her conviction that ordinary perception and work are of the same nature and value as scientific and other forms of specialized and elitist knowledge' (in Weil, 1987, p. 7):

> And as for knowing my own being, what I am is defined by what I can do. So there is one thing I can know: myself. And I cannot know anything else. To know is to know what I can do; and I know to the degree that I substitute 'to act' and 'to be acted upon' for 'to enjoy,' 'to suffer,' 'to feel,' and 'to imagine.' In this way I transform illusion into certainty and chance into necessity. (Weil, 1987, p. 59)

A theme Weil shared with Descartes is the search for a method of knowledge or epistemology likely to yield 'truth', that is, likely to result in knowledge about which one could be certain. Like Descartes, Weil found a pivotal role for doubt, because she saw all too clearly how easily people could deceive themselves by accepting common knowledge uncritically. Her statements on self-deception are unequivocal on this point:

> It is true that simple belief succeeds very well in having the power of certitude when it is at white heat from the fire of collective feelings, yet it remains belief for all that. Its force is illusory. (Weil, 1957, p. 165)

> I have an extremely severe standard for intellectual honesty, so severe that I never met anyone who did not seem to fall short of it in more than one respect; and I am always afraid of failing in it myself. (Weil, 1977, p. 14)

> The truth is hidden. . . . The truth is not revealed except in nakedness . . . which means the rupture of all those attachments which for each human being constitute the reason for living; those whom

he loves, public esteem and possessions, material and moral, all that. (Weil, 1957, p. 82)

Genius is the supernatural virtue of humility in the domain of thought. (Weil, 1970, p. 335)

The intelligent man who is proud of his intelligence is like a con-demned man who is proud of his large cell. (Weil, 1981, p. 29)

What is generally named egoism is not love of self, it is a defect of perspective. (Weil, 1957, p. 133)

The massacre of one hundred thousand Chinese hardly alters the order of the world as they perceive it, but if instead a fellow worker has a slight rise in pay which they have not, the order of the world is turned upside down! This is not love of self, it is that men, being finite creatures, only apply the idea of legitimate order to the immediate neighbourhood of their hearts. (Weil, 1957, p. 133)

Weil shared another characteristic with Descartes: she pos-tulated a dual structure to the universe and differentiated 'mind' from 'body'. Weil did not advance a strict dichotomy between these domains, however, and understood clearly that there existed a two-way interaction between them: physiological con-ditions affect mental states, and mental states affect physiological functioning. Thus, her position is perhaps under-stood best as one of 'limited' or 'attributive' dualism: a view that recognizes two distinct sets of properties or attributes essential to the human condition. Even if these properties ultimately are found to reflect two facets of a single reality, it is important to maintain the distinction between them and to refuse to reduce one to the other prematurely. Although Weil did not succeed in demonstrating how these opposing tendencies ultimately unite in a common substance, neither have current philosophers or scientists succeeded in doing so.

Aside from the implications of Weil's dualism in her search for religious truth, which we cover in later chapters, Weil's philosophical position prevented her from lapsing into three contemporary maladies: scientism – an exaggerated worship of science and scientific method, coupled with a reductionist belief that science can answer all questions of human concern; specialization – the notion that inquiry should proceed by pursuing narrowly defined problems circumscribed by extremely tight boundaries; and technophilia – a stance that shifts science from the pursuit of knowledge to a role of handmaiden to utility, commerce and consumer society.

It is fashionable in some intellectual circles to relegate dualism to the domain of the superstitious and to imply that such a metaphysical position is inherently unscientific. This judgement overlooks the fact that the position of physical monism is ultimately no more defensible than that of dualism. One can adopt a non-physical monism, because a philosophical adherence to monism does not necessarily imply the corollary of materialism, nor does Weil's brand of attributive dualism preclude other philosophical possibilities, such as a philosophical pluralism. In short, the reductionist approach to science is often assumed with an air of authority once reserved for theological pronouncements, even though the philosophy of science literature confirms that the scientific approach is much more complex than the slogans of science. The broad trend of scholars is away from seeing science as 'Truth' to conceptualizing it as one perspective among a variety of ways of knowing. More to the point here, a broad range of feminist analyses of traditional objectivist epistemologies overlap those of Weil, thus placing her criticism of scientism as a forerunner of these recent writings.

Weil's critique of science points to a key distinction between venerating science as one possible and enriching way of knowing versus worshipping science as the only avenue to truth (scientism). She also cautions against a monolithic view of science that fails to see its organic growth and development over time, one of the surest proofs of its fallibility and its inherent limitations at any given moment in history:

Science has become the most modern form of the consciousness of man who has not yet found himself or has once again lost himself, to apply Marx's telling dictum concerning religion. (Weil, 1973, p. 35)

In our days, when . . . scientists have so oddly usurped the place of priests, the public acknowledges, with a totally unjustified docility, that the artistic and scientific faculties are sacred. This is generally felt to be self-evident, though it is very far from being so. (Weil, 1962, p. 13)

The nineteenth-century cult of science consisted in the belief that the science of the period, by means of a simple development in certain directions already defined by the results achieved, would provide a definite answer to all the problems that could present themselves to man, without exception. What has, in fact, happened is that science, after expanding a little, has itself 'cracked up.' The science in favour today, although derived from the former, is a different science. Nineteenth-century science has been reverently deposited in the museum under the label 'classical science.' (Weil, 1973, pp. 170–1)

One could count on one's fingers the number of scientists throughout the world with a general idea of the history and development of their particular science: there is none who is really competent as regards sciences other than his own. As science forms an indivisible whole, one may say that there are no longer, strictly speaking, scientists, but only unskilled hands doing scientific work, cogs in a whole their minds are quite incapable of embracing. (Weil, 1973, p. 13)

The disappearance of scientific truth appears to our eyes as the disappearance of truth, thanks to our habit of mistaking the one for the other. So soon as truth disappears, utility at once takes its place, because man always directs his effort towards some good or other. Thus utility becomes something which the intelligence is no longer entitled to define or to judge, but only to serve. (Weil, 1968, p. 63)

Having identified the crisis of classical science, Weil goes on to say that even if classical science could embrace the whole universe, its rendering would still be limited because its vantage point is partial, incomplete:

> The universe it describes is a slave's universe, and man, including slaves, is not wholly a slave. (Weil, 1968, p. 11)

> Classical science is limited in range because the human mind is limited. (Weil, 1968, p. 11)

> Therefore classical science is without beauty; it neither touches the heart nor contains any wisdom. It is understandable that Keats[1] hated Newton, and that Goethe did not love him either. (Weil, 1968, p. 16)

Weil views suspiciously the connection between science and technology because it compromises the supposed disinterest of the true scientist, and she also questions the uses which are made of the discoveries of technical science. She calls on Western civilization to question its pride in the accomplishments of science, as well as questioning the fundamental social constructions of truth and progress:

> Technical application plays such a large part in the prestige of science that one would be inclined to expect savants to derive a powerful stimulant from reflecting upon the different forms of application. In fact, what provides a stimulant is not that but the actual prestige such applications confer on science. Just as the idea of making history goes to the heads of politicians, so the savants become intoxicated at feeling themselves to be taking part in something really great. Great in the sense of false greatness, certainly; a greatness independent of any consideration for the good. (Weil, 1952, p. 255)

> Were it not for its technical applications, no member of the public today would take any interest in science; and if the public didn't take an interest in science, those who follow a scientific career would have had to choose another one. They have no right to take up the detached attitude which they do. (Weil, 1952, p. 256)

> The savants insist that the public should regard science with that religious respect which is owed to truth, and the public accepts to

do so. But it is being deceived. Science is not a fruit of the spirit of truth, and this is obvious as soon as one looks into the matter. (Weil, 1952, p. 251)

The primary social consideration for savants is purely and simply one of professional duty. Savants are people who are paid to manufacture science; they are expected to manufacture some; they feel it to be their duty to manufacture some. But that is insufficient for them as a stimulant. Professional advancement, professorships, rewards of all kinds, honors and money, receptions abroad, the esteem and admiration of colleagues, reputation, fame, titles – all that counts for a great deal. (Weil, 1952, pp. 256–7)

While Weil believes that scientific inquiry and the desire for truth are not synonymous and that science cannot rescue humanity from self-deception, from the tyranny of subjectivity, she does not simply collapse into the nihilism (or solipsism) of Gorgias[2] and the Sophists. She maintains the necessity of remaining sceptical of collective thought, while at the same time arguing in favour of the communal welfare.

Notes

1 Weil may have meant Blake here.

2 Gorgias of Leontini (*c.* 483–376 BC) was an early Greek philosopher who argued that reality, or 'Being', was unknowable and ineffable. His argument is generally regarded as precursory to the Sophist position.

2
The Individual and the Collective
Distortion of Self

Aristotle declared that man 'is by nature a political animal' and that 'an individual who is unsocial naturally and not accidentally is either beneath our notice or more than human' (Aristotle, *Politics*, *c.* 328 BC). In characteristic fashion, Weil begins with a similar belief – that humans are rooted in the social order – only to follow the thought with one that is quite contradictory: 'the social is irremediably the domain of the devil' (Weil, 1951a, p. 54). This declaration seems to place Weil in the tradition of Jean-Jacques Rousseau, who articulated the concept of the 'noble savage' and reversed the doctrine of Original Sin: humans are born good and then corrupted by the social order. Weil's statements sometimes echo this position:

> The social order . . . is essentially evil, whatever it may be. (Weil, 1973, p. 146)

What frightens me is the Church as a social structure. Not only on account of its blemishes, but from the very fact that it is something social. (Weil, 1951a, p. 52)

Only fanatics are able to set no value on their own existence save to the extent that it serves a collective cause; to react against the subordination of the individual to the collectivity implies that one begins by refusing to subordinate one's own destiny to the course of history. (Weil, 1973, p. 124)

The needs of a human being are sacred. Their satisfaction cannot be subordinated either to reasons of state, or to any consideration of money, nationality, race, or colour, or to the moral or other value attributed to the human being in question, or to any consideration whatsoever.
   There is no legitimate limit to the satisfaction of the needs of a human being except as imposed by necessity and by the needs of other human beings. (Weil, 1962, p. 224)

Idolatry is the name of the error which attributes a sacred character to the collectivity; and it is the commonest of crimes, at all times, at all places. (Weil, 1981, p. 18)

Unless I am mistaken, it has never been suggested that Christ died to save nations. (Weil, 1952, p. 131)

In reading further, however, one sees why Weil's thinking is not easily categorized, for even while she echoes the Rousseauistic position, she balances it with a vivid recognition that human beings are quite capable of independent evil – evil that stems from the personal order. Weil holds that 'there is no form of cruelty or depravity of which ordinary, decent people are not capable, once the corresponding psychological mechanisms have been set in motion' (1952, p. 112). In an intellectual vein similar to Goethe's literature, Schopenhauer's philosophy and Freud's psychology, Weil paints a conflictual portrait of the individual: a person is both drawn toward the 'good' and pushed toward the 'evil', even where the power of social influence is held constant. Weil writes, in *Oppression and Liberty*, that 'the essential contradiction in human life is that man, with a straining after the good constituting his very being, is at the same time subject in his entire being, both in mind and in flesh, to a blind force, to a necessity completely indifferent to the good. So it is; and that is why no human thinking can escape from contradiction' (Weil, 1973, p. 173).

Weil's thought reflects this duality at a number of levels. When speaking at a psychological level, she often uses as metaphors the language of grace and gravity; when operating at a social level of analysis, she contrasts the individual and the collective; when addressing duality at a philosophical level, she contrasts freedom with necessity; and when dealing with primarily religious issues, she contrasts God with the carnal world:

> It is only by directing my thoughts towards something better than myself that I am drawn upwards by this something . . . . What is thus brought about by thought direction is in no way comparable to suggestion. . . . Contradiction is the criterion. We cannot by suggestion obtain things which are incompatible. Only grace can do that. A sensitive person who by suggestion becomes courageous hardens himself; often he may even, by a sort of savage pleasure, amputate his own sensitivity. Grace alone can give courage while leaving the sensitivity intact, or sensitivity while leaving the courage intact. (Weil, 1963, pp. 90–2)

> [The world is ruled by necessity, a] blind mechanism [which] . . . continually tosses men about . . .
> If the mechanism were not blind there would not be any affliction. Affliction is anonymous before all things; it deprives its victims of their personality and makes them into things. It is indifferent; and it is the coldness of this indifference – a metallic coldness – that freezes all those it touches right to the depths of their souls. . . .
> Affliction would not have this power without the element of chance contained by it. (Weil, 1951a, pp. 124–5)

> Everything points to the fact that, unless supernatural grace intervenes, there is no form of cruelty or depravity of which ordinary, decent people are not capable, once the corresponding psychological mechanisms have been set in motion. (Weil, 1952, p. 112)

Men have the same carnal nature as animals. If a hen is hurt, the others rush upon it, attacking it with their beaks. This phenomenon is as automatic as gravitation. (Weil, 1951a, p. 122)

In discussing the proper relationship between the individual and society, Weil ends up at a decidedly interactionist position regarding self-development. That is, she believes that both personal (innate) and social (learned) factors are minimally required for healthy development and declares that 'a human being has roots by virtue of his real, active, and natural participation in the life of a community' (Weil, 1952, p. 43). Further, even the spiritual dimension may be essential to achieve a release from one's chains. According to Weil, the essential step for bridging the individual and social domains is connecting thought to action. A broad range of themes inherent in Weil's work – contradiction as a truth criterion, the proper status of manual labour, criticism of classical science, and the method of attention – all hinge on Weil's search for a balanced relation between thought and action:

[C]omplete, unlimited freedom of expression . . . , without the least restriction or reserve, is an absolute need on the part of the intelligence. It follows from this that it is a need of the soul, for when the intelligence is ill-at-ease the whole soul is sick [dis-eased].[1] (Weil, 1952, p. 23)

What is evil about the social element, then, becomes possible to isolate. When a social structure not only constrains thinking, but even glorifies the power used to exercise such constraints, Weil sees the social order as the domain of the devil, the epitome of evil:

Today, science, history, politics, the organization of labor, religion even, . . . offer nothing to men's minds except brute force. Such is our civilization. It is a tree that bears the fruit it deserves. (Weil, 1952, p. 295)

Our conception of greatness is the very one that has inspired Hitler's whole life. When we denounce it without the remotest recognition of its application to ourselves, the angels must either cry or laugh, if there happens to be angels who interest themselves in our propaganda. (Weil, 1952, p. 219)

The only punishment capable of punishing Hitler, and deterring little boys thirsting for greatness in coming centuries from following his example is such a total transformation of the meaning attached to greatness that he should thereby be excluded from it. (Weil, 1952, p. 227)

Simone Weil believes that a harmonious solution to the problem of the individual and the collective is provided by intelligence. For her, 'the position of the intelligence is the key to this harmony', one which exists only where intelligence 'can be exercised without hindrance and can reach the complete fulfillment of its function'. Intelligence 'requires total liberty, implying the right to deny everything, and allowing of no domination' (Weil, 1951a, p. 78). Whatever stifles complete freedom of speculative thought places people in chains. Just as the method of attention must be sustained without regard for results, so 'a perfect thought is an independent thought and nothing else'. For Weil, no thought can be deemed unworthy of being entertained: 'True liberty is . . . defined by a relationship between thought and action; the absolutely free man would be he whose every action proceeded from a preliminary judgment concerning the end which he set himself and the sequence of means suitable for attaining this end' (Weil, 1973, p. 85).

Because Weil views the power and influence of the group as disproportionate *vis-à-vis* the individual, one must consciously emphasize the primacy of the individual in order to counterbalance the weight of collective influence. For Weil, whenever human beings work as passive instruments to fulfil a collective need, carrying out actions that ensue from ideas other than their own or other than those that they have made their own, the result is oppression. This line of reasoning suggests that the social order itself, to the extent that it allows or encourages independent thinking, actually *promotes* development in the Aristotelian sense, by placing proper limits on narcissistic individualism. As Weil goes on to say, wherever the intelligence 'usurps control there is an excess of individualism. Wherever it is hampered or uneasy there is an oppressive collectivism, or several of them' (Weil, 1951a, p. 78). As Weil surveys humanity and its collective history, however, she finds precious little evidence of such an intellectually fertile or vibrant social context. In contrast to historical example, she describes an ideal social environment as one that offers maximum freedom and independence:

> [T]he least evil society is that in which the general run of men are most often obliged to think while acting, have the most opportunities for exercising control over collective life as a whole, and enjoy the greatest amount of independence. (Weil, 1973, p. 103)

> [T]he idea of labour considered as a human value is doubtless the one and only spiritual conquest achieved by the human mind since the miracle of Greece; this was perhaps the only gap in the ideal of human life elaborated by Greece and left behind by her as an undying heritage. (Weil, 1973, p. 106)

> The human soul has need of truth and of freedom of expression. (Weil, 1981, p. 11)

> Suppose the devil were bargaining for the soul of some poor wretch and someone, moved by pity, should step in and say to the devil: 'It is a shame for you to bid so low; the commodity is worth at least twice as much.'
> Such is the sinister farce which has been played by the working-class movement, its trade unions, its political parties, its leftist intellectuals. (Weil, 1981, p. 22)

> [W]hat can those do who still persist, against all eventualities, in honouring human dignity both in themselves and in others? Nothing, except endeavour to introduce a little play into the cogs of the machine that is grinding us down; seize every opportunity of

awakening a little thought wherever they are able; encourage whatever is capable, in the sphere of politics, economics or technique, of
leaving the individual here and there a certain freedom of movement amid the trammels cast around him by the social organization.
(Weil, 1973, p. 121)

Weil does acknowledge the necessity for certain natural constraints on freedom, which she defines in mental rather than
purely physical terms:

> The liberty of men of good will, though limited in the sphere of
> action, is complete in that of conscience. For, having incorporated
> the rules into their own being, the prohibited possibilities no longer
> present themselves to the mind, and have not to be rejected. Just as
> the habit, formed by education, of not eating disgusting or danger-
> ous things is not felt by the normal man to be any limitation of his
> liberty in the domain of food. Only a child feels such a limitation.
> (Weil, 1952, p. 13)

> It is clear enough that one kind of work differs substantially from
> another by reason of something which has nothing to do with wel-
> fare, or leisure, or security, and yet which claims each man's
> devotion; a fisherman battling against wind and waves in his little
> boat, although he suffers from cold, fatigue, lack of leisure and even
> of sleep, danger and a primitive level of existence, has a more envi-
> able lot than the manual worker on a production-line, who is
> nevertheless better off as regards nearly all these matters. That is
> because his work resembles far more the work of a free man,
> despite the fact that routine and blind improvisation sometimes play
> a fairly large part in it. The craftsman of the Middle Ages also occu-
> pies, from this point of view, a fairly honourable position, although
> the 'tricks of the trade' which play so large a part in all work carried
> out by hand are to a great extent something blind; as for the fully
> skilled worker, trained in modern technical methods, he perhaps
> resembles most closely the perfect workman. (Weil, 1973, pp.
> 100–1)

Where the social order does not allow independent thinking, the primary rationale of its institutions can be categorized
as power and its primary method, force. Even if only one person

is silenced by the social order, then the society is unjust and the one self is destined to become a distorted self. Weil's aversion to the use of force, which includes both overt aggression and covert oppression, is one of the clearest patterns that emerges from both her work and her life – and especially in her comments on politics and religion. In these two domains in particular, Weil argues for a definite need to achieve congruence of thought and action. But how does one go about this crucial task of connecting thought to action? One answer, for Simone Weil, is commitment to method, but method animated by a desire for truth, and not method as a technique defined by a particular intellectual discipline. The method she proposes is one that can animate all knowing, be it in the domain of science, religion, art or daily life. This approach to knowing is what Weil calls *attente* (attention), a state wherein one is willing to remain on the border between wanting to know and not knowing.

Note

1 The connection between 'ill-at-ease' or 'dis-ease' and the modern term for sickness: disease.

3

The Method of Attention
Construction of Self

Weil's thought cuts across many disciplines – from science and religion to art and history, from philosophy and psychology to literature and poetry. Part of the reason for this range stems from her refusal to see 'Truth' as defined by any one field or intellectual lens, whether scientific, philosophical, or anything else. Her work and life reflect an individual committed to remaining between boundaries intellectually as well as socially, an individual who recognized that intellectual disciplines in isolation from each other afford only limited glimpses of reality. Weil also recognizes that disciplinary loyalists argue incessantly over method in the narrow sense of the term, method as technique. In their most polemical moments, these disciplinary proponents assert that it is the particular technique that guarantees objectivity and thus assures the truth of a given set of findings.

Weil understood the fallacy of such contentions, recognizing that methods are tools, techniques of inquiry, that are ultimately only as good as the skill of the user when applied to problems that are meaningful. Weil argued that to choose what to study presupposes a certain sensibility, and that one needs to have some sense of what one is looking for even to know where to begin looking. Indeed, 'looking', knowing where and how to look, comprise important tenets of her thought. Further, Weil insists that desire (love) for a piece of reality is a prerequisite to all authentic inquiry. She argued that every inquirer must make critical decisions about where to look, how to recognize what one desires, and where to direct one's attention. In the search for 'Truth' it is best to begin at precisely this point, at the point where we ask what in life is worthy of attending to, and indeed how to know that something is worthy of attention prior to attending to it.

The method of attention

Weil's focus is the process of attention itself, a level of analysis that cuts across mere tools of inquiry and across the intellectual constructions of disciplines. She sees attention as critical to all areas of human endeavour, from science and philosophy to education and religious studies, and from areas of intellectual inquiry to the arena of physical labour:

> Attention consists of suspending our thought, leaving it detached, empty, and ready to be penetrated by the object. . . . Above all our thought should be empty, waiting, not seeking anything, but ready to receive in its naked truth the object that is to penetrate it. (Weil, 1951a, pp. 111–12)

> After months of inward darkness, I suddenly had the everlasting conviction that any human being, even though practically devoid of natural faculties, can penetrate to the kingdom of truth reserved for genius, if only he longs for truth and perpetually concentrates all his attention upon its attainment. (Weil, 1951a, p. 64)

> We do not obtain the most precious gifts by going in search of them but by waiting for them. (Weil, 1951a, p. 112)

Although people seem to be unaware of it today, the development of the faculty of attention forms the real object and almost the sole interest of studies. (Weil, 1977, p. 45)

Students must therefore work without any wish to gain good marks, to pass examinations, to win school successes; without any reference to their natural abilities and tastes; applying themselves equally to all their tasks, with the idea that each one will help to form in them the habit of . . . attention. (Weil, 1977, p. 46)

Willpower, the kind that, if need be, makes us set our teeth and endure suffering, is the principal weapon of the apprentice engaged in manual work. But, contrary to the usual belief, it has practically no place in study. The intelligence can only be led by desire. For there to be desire, there must be pleasure and joy in the work. The intelligence only grows and bears fruit in joy. The joy of learning is as indispensable in study as breathing is in running. Where it is lacking there are no real students, but only poor caricatures of apprentices who, at the end of their apprenticeship, will not even have a trade. (Weil, 1977, p. 48)

A village idiot in the literal sense of the word, if he really loves truth, is infinitely superior to Aristotle in his thought, even though he never utters anything but inarticulate murmurs. (Weil, 1977, p. 329)

The true road exists. Plato and many others have followed it. But it is open only to those who, recognizing themselves to be incapable of finding it, give up looking for it, and yet do not cease to desire it to the exclusion of everything else. (Weil, 1973, p. 157)

The intelligence can be exercised in three ways. It can work on technical problems, that is to say, discover means to achieve an already given objective. It can provide light when a choice lies before the will concerning the path to be followed. Finally, it can operate alone, separately from the other faculties, in a purely theoretical speculation where all question of action has been provisionally set aside. (Weil, 1952, p. 23)

It is uniquely the desire . . . [for beauty]. This desire, given a certain degree of intensity and of purity, is the same thing as genius. At all levels it is the same thing as attention. If this were understood, . . .

one would realize that the intelligence functions only in joy. (Weil, 1957, p. 123)

Because affliction and truth need the same kind of attention before they can be heard, the spirit of justice and the spirit of truth are one. The spirit of justice and truth is nothing else but a certain kind of attention, which is pure love. (Weil, 1962, p. 28)

In considering the last two statements, one can understand that Weil's notion of attention seems closest to her 'third way' of exercising intelligence. Achieving the proper state for this exercise of intelligence may be arduous, but it is also the state most likely to produce insight into the nature of truth. Why do so few seekers travel the path of inquiry through the method of attention? According to Weil, the way of attention is so incredibly demanding that few can endure it. For example, where contradictory statements both seem valid, one must endure the tension of contradictory truths:

[I]f both must be accepted [two incompatible thoughts], the contradiction must then be recognized as a fact. It must then be used as a two-limbed tool, like a pair of pincers. . . . But . . . there is a legitimate and an illegitimate use of contradiction.

The illegitimate use lies in coupling together incompatible thoughts as if they were compatible. The legitimate use lies, first of all, when two incompatible thoughts present themselves to the mind, in exhausting all the powers of the intellect in an attempt to eliminate at least one of them. If this is impossible, [then] both must be accepted. . . .

Contradiction itself, far from always being a criterion of error, is sometimes a sign of truth. Plato knew this. (Weil, 1973, p. 173)

This facet of Weil's thought provides an important key to understanding her life: she fervently believed that the greatest barrier to truth was premature closure and that 'comforting beliefs' are seldom rational (Weil, 1973, p. 43). For Weil, all wrong translations, absurdities, faulty connections, cherished illusions and misunderstandings 'are due to the fact that thought has seized upon some idea too hastily, and being thus prematurely blocked, is not open to the truth' (Weil, 1951a, p. 112). Comfort is a driving force for most people, and it leads them to put on visors that so block the field of vision that they are rendered blind to truth, a point made by Perrin and Thibon in their discussion of Weil's thought:

> She considered all social privileges – money, rank, honours, influence, etc. – to be screens between the soul and reality, deceiving us as much as they promote our comfort. She saw them as a kind of padding made of illusions and preventing man from having real contact with necessity in its naked truth. (Perrin and Thibon, 1953, pp. 1–2)

The life of Simone Weil, to the extent that it runs counter to the ordinary urge for comfort and closure, confronts us with the notion that there are no shortcuts to perceiving reality accurately. Further, her life suggests that resisting premature closure or easy retreat into one or another disciplinary box requires a great effort of attention and resistance to natural inclinations: 'Something in our soul has a far more violent repugnance for true attention than the flesh has for bodily fatigue' (Weil, 1951a, p. 111). To understand clearly the challenge Weil is confronting us with, consider the life an athlete must live in order to become a contender for an Olympic gold medal: the years of daily struggle and workout, the attention to diet and nutrition, the guiding hand of a coach or mentor, the minimizing of ordinary social pursuits like friendship, family life or a non-athletic career, and the uncertainty that concentrated effort and devotion will ultimately succeed. Weil's painful example suggests that becoming an Olympic gold medalist is *easy* compared to becoming an accurate perceiver of reality.

Most people would ask, 'Why worry about it? Why pay such a high price merely to perceive one moment of reality accurately?' It may be that answers to these linked questions become the criteria by which the life of Simone Weil is best judged. Weil offers some possible answers. She calls for a mind that becomes 'open to the truth' in order to avoid errors in understanding (Weil, 1951a, p. 112). She believes that much of what people identify as 'evil', 'fate', and 'the world as it is' is rooted in human ignorance or misunderstanding – the source of which is lack of attention rather than lack of intellectual ability. Weil asks the question: 'Is not evil analogous to illusion?' (Weil, 1977, p. 383). For Weil, many unfavourable social conditions that distort human lives are really symptoms of a failure of attention. They result from ignorance and self-constructed illusions and delusions that reflect the human tendency to arrive at closure quickly and prematurely. A life of attention receives its rewards simply by alleviating some of the unhealthy or evil conditions arising primarily from human ignorance. Weil believes that anything 'that contributes towards giving those who are at the bottom of the social scale the feeling that they possess a value' runs counter to the direction of brute force (Weil, 1973, p. 145). While some authors (and even Weil herself) label these facets of her thought 'utopian' (see McLellan, 1990), Weil challenges readers to counter the statement 'Such is the world' with the statement 'Such have we made the world.' Weil asserts that if humanity is intricately involved in constructing the social world, then it could (and should) construct it more carefully and intentionally:

> No doubt all this is purely utopian. But to give even a summary description of a state of things which would be better than what actually exists is always to build a utopia; yet nothing is more necessary to our life than such descriptions, provided it is always reason that is responsible for them. (Weil, 1973, p. 106)

Before discounting Weil's views as utopian, critics might consider her thought in the light of William James's work. It is clear that the work of James informed the thinking of Weil, as she explicitly cites it in her journal (e.g. Weil, 1970, p. 26). Like Weil, James focused on the import of attention, limiting the term to a more precise psychological sense by referring to those stimuli to which we attend at the expense of competing stimuli which we ignore. A thing may be present to a person a thousand times, but if it goes completely unnoticed by the individual, it cannot be said to enter her experience. A person's 'empirical thought depends on the things he has experienced, but what these shall be is to a large extent determined by his habits of attention' (James, 1890/1950, p. 286). Thus, James concludes that all of our consciousness – our sense of meaning, our very sense of self – must be constructed from material to which we have attended. The *meaning* we derive as we experience life, the *consciousness* that is a stream of this ongoing experience, and the *self* that we construct as a personal representation of consciousness are all dependent upon our habits of attention.

What we pay attention to becomes the stuff from which the self is constructed. What we choose to attend to or absorb is who we are. Simone Weil recognized this connection and its complication: many of the things that we pay attention to receive our notice as a result of social influence. We have learned or been conditioned to pay attention to certain things at the expense of others, to see reality a certain way, because we attend only to a few fragments perceptually available to us. When Weil speaks of becoming a self in terms of 'decreation', then, it is important to understand her statements in this context. To perceive reality accurately, one of the most difficult things is to unlearn what has been taught, to eliminate conditioned habits of attention in order to develop new ones. Anyone who has ever tried to break even a simple habit, like hand-wringing, nail-biting or knuckle-popping, understands the energy and constant effort required to act in a direction counter to the habit. Where habits are more complex, such as patterns of eating or of interacting socially, they seem almost impossible to break. Thus, her reference to 'emptying' the self to maintain attention does not mean a total 'lack of self'; it is more akin to emptying the self of culturally conditioned preconceptions and biases that skew attempts to make more direct contact with a piece of reality. It may be that the phenomenological emphasis on 'bracketing' one's biases and preconceptions comes close to Weil's intellectual manoeuvres here. Indeed, a statement by Merleau-Ponty may best capture the stance toward which Weil is working – a notion of attention as 'circumscribed' ignorance:

> Empiricism cannot see that we need to know what we are looking for, otherwise we would not be looking for it, and intellectualism fails to see that we need to be ignorant of what we are looking for, or equally again we should not be searching. They are in agreement in that neither . . . attaches due importance to that circumscribed ignorance, that still 'empty' but already determinate intention which is attention itself. (Merleau-Ponty, 1962, p. 28)

Weil describes this process of breaking out of the habitual in order to understand the viewpoints of others:

> I have the essential need, and I think I can say the vocation, to move among men of every class and complexion, mixing with them and sharing their life and outlook, so far that is to say as conscience allows, merging into the crowd and disappearing among them, so that they show themselves as they are, putting off all disguises with me. . . . (Weil, 1951a, p. 48)

> As for me, on the contrary, as I think I told you, I have the germ of all possible crimes, or nearly all, within me. (Weil, 1951a, p. 48)

> Except the seed die. . . . It has to die in order to liberate the energy it bears within it so that with this energy new forms may be developed.
> So we have to die in order to liberate a tied up energy, in order to possess an energy which is free and capable of understanding the true relationship of things. (Weil, 1951a, p. 30)

Given Weil's understanding of attention, the social role of the saint, artist or rebel is to attend to facets of reality that run 'counter' to the direction of those things on which we focus as a result of social conditioning. By first attending to how people 'of every class and complexion' perceive reality, one can better understand alternative readings of reality. By following these alternative perceptions with congruent actions, we can actually shape our social reality, rather than simply be shaped by it. In Weil's terms, we must first empty the self, then remain in a state of attentive waiting, in order to be filled by possibilities that can lead us in a direction more likely to actualize human potential.

Filling the self: art, love and beauty

According to Weil, the path of attention is the way toward truth, and one must embark upon this path with as little emotional and intellectual baggage as possible. Her emphasis on deconstruction of the self – as prerequisite to reconstructing or reshaping oneself – may be understood as dumping the baggage: one must first empty the self in order to be filled again by the fruits that germinate from one's state of attention. Even then, Weil adds a caveat: you must accept the risk of emptying the self, only to be left in a state of emptiness. Results are not guaranteed; thus, you must remain in a willing state of attention without regard for results. The value she places on this willing state of emptiness explains why she believes a village idiot who loves truth is superior to Aristotle, why she maintains 'the true road . . . is open only to those who, recognizing themselves to be incapable of finding it, give up looking for it, and yet do not cease to desire it' (Weil, 1973, p. 157), and why 'students must . . . work without any wish to gain good marks, to pass examinations, to win school successes' (Weil, 1977, p. 46).

With this emphasis, Weil is explicitly rejecting utilitarian and pragmatic criteria of judgement; in their place, she values the path itself. A person must be content to wait in a state of attention, without regard for results, and with no certain knowledge of potential outcomes. Weil emphasizes that one cannot know where the path leads, or what fruits it will bear, if one refuses to stay on it long enough to find out. Simone Weil's life testifies to her belief that a life of attention and waiting is inevitably a life of risk; no one can know where it will lead or what results will ensue. To refuse to take the risk, though, has premature closure as its price. By putting arbitrary limits on what they will attend to, people risk cutting themselves off from dimensions of life that may be the most valuable ones available. Much of Weil's work expresses admiration for those she describes as perceptually open, as embarking on paths that may lead nowhere, as taking part in activities because they are fulfilling and satisfying in and of themselves. And when Weil speaks of love, art and beauty, she stresses that each of these domains must be attended to 'without regard' for results:

Beauty is the harmony of chance and the good. (Weil, 1977, p. 377)

The conditions of intellectual or artistic creation are so intimate and secret that no one can penetrate into them from outside. (Weil, 1951a, p. 86)

The beautiful is a carnal attraction which keeps us at a distance and implies a renunciation. . . . We want to eat all the other objects of desire. The beautiful is that which we desire without wishing to eat it. (Weil, 1977, p. 378)

We have to remain quite still and unite ourselves with that which we desire yet do not approach. (Weil, 1977, p. 378)

Beauty excludes selfish ends. (Weil, 1957, p. 104)

Beauty is a fruit which we look at without trying to seize it. (Weil, 1977, p. 379)

Of a perfect poem one can say only that each word is in the place where it is absolutely appropriate to be. (Weil, 1957, p. 104)

[As] soon as truth disappears, utility at once takes its place, because man always directs his effort towards some good or other.

Thus utility becomes something which the intelligence is no longer entitled to define or to judge, but only to serve. (Weil, 1968, p. 63)

Note that Weil does not view beauty or love as separable from the pain and affliction of human experience; to do so would involve evaluation by outcome:

If we want to have a love which will protect the soul from wounds, we must love something other than God. (Weil, 1977, p. 358)

It is only necessary to know that love is an orientation and not a state of the soul. Anyone who does not know this will fall into despair at the first onset of affliction.
[In affliction, a person] . . . quivers like a butterfly pinned alive to a tray. But throughout the horror he can go on wanting to love. (Weil, 1977, p. 452)

Beauty is a fruit which we look at without trying to seize it.
The same with an affliction which we contemplate without drawing back. (Weil, 1977, p. 379)

In the beauty of the world brute necessity becomes an object of love. What is more beautiful than the action of gravity on the fugitive folds of the sea waves, or on the almost eternal folds of the mountains?
The sea is not less beautiful in our eyes because we know that sometimes ships are wrecked by it. On the contrary, this adds to its beauty. (Weil, 1951a, pp. 128–9)

The extreme affliction which overtakes human beings does not create human misery, it merely reveals it. (Weil, 1977, p. 389)

Although some critics might see Weil's life as a manifestation of Freud's theory of sublimation, she herself explicitly rejected this notion along with most of Freud's other ideas. She did, however, acknowledge the validity of one of his claims: 'Every attachment is of the same nature as sexuality. In that, Freud is right (but only that)' (Weil, 1970, p. 287). Continuing, she wrote that 'in Plato's eyes carnal love is a degraded image of true love.

Chaste human love (conjugal fidelity) is a less degraded image of it. Only in the stupidity of the present day could the idea of sublimation arise' (Weil, 1977, p. 358). In any case, Weil's passion for equality, freedom and truth far exceeded her pursuit of sexual attachment – regardless of how one interprets the origin or basis of her passion. For the most part she was firm and without regrets in renouncing sexual involvement, although she feared being the 'barren fig tree' (Weil, 1951a, p. 46f.). And even when speaking of herself as a 'barren fig tree', she referred not to fertility in terms of traditional child-bearing; rather, she was concerned that her ideas would not bear fruit if people discredited them because of the inadequacy or peculiarity of the messenger.

4

Balancing Equality and Freedom
Labour and Politics

The production and consumption mentality which was gaining prominence at the beginning of the twentieth century had ramifications at every level of society. Weil and her contemporaries had already seen the pernicious effects of mass production and the objectification of human beings during and following World War I. As people became more distanced and alienated from their products, the results of their labour became less visibly connected to their source. In the case of warfare, mechanization removed killers so far from their victims that individuals were able to slaughter on a mass level with relatively few pangs of guilt because they could not really see the results of their actions. Weil, like a good philosopher, seeks to understand the root causes of the phenomena she witnessed in horror during the years after World War I.

One of Weil's first forays into political thought occurs in an essay, 'Reflexions sur les causes de la liberté et de l'oppression sociale', a title which suggests that oppression should be addressed through a more profound understanding of social change. She describes an ideal society, calling on thinkers to pursue goals that coincide with actual circumstances and to do so by analysing concrete problems rigorously: 'What is required is not only searching, rigorous thinking, subjected, so as to avoid all possibility of error, to the most exacting checking, but also historical, technical and scientific investigations of an unparalleled range and precision, and conducted from an entirely new point of view' (Weil, 1973, p. 60).

Weil did not envision revolution as an ultimate goal, as did Marx, because she saw that all movements grounded in force were ultimately corrupt, no matter how noble the end goal might be. Instead, she insisted on a strict adherence to the 'conditions of existence' in proposing reforms. The ability of reformers to enact and preserve social, political and industrial change depends on the extent to which their reforms conform to necessity, to actual conditions of existence.

Weil identifies certain groups as holding disproportionate power in society, including the military, technicians, economists, bankers, priests, and specialists in coordinating groups in government and private sectors ('executives'). Further, she maintains that a significant factor in perpetuating oppression is the struggle to obtain and retain power. One of her main objections to power as a *means* to achieve some end, worthy or not, is that it inevitably suppresses thinking – a condition exemplified in the mindless support and docile acceptance of Hitler by his followers:

> The problem is, therefore, quite clear; it is a question of knowing whether it is possible to conceive of an organization of production which, though powerless to remove the necessities imposed by nature and the social constraint arising therefrom, would enable these at any rate to be exercised without grinding down souls and bodies under oppression. . . . If we can manage to conceive in concrete terms the conditions of this liberating organization, then it only remains for us to exercise, in order to move towards it, all the powers of action, small or great, at our disposal. (Weil, 1973, p. 56)

Simone Weil's work in the factories of Paris revolutionized her thinking on labour and politics in several ways, the most significant being her assessment of the chances for a proletarian revolt among French workers, which she tellingly described as practically nil: 'I think it is only the bourgeois who could have any illusion in this matter' (Weil, 1965, p. 35). For Weil, work should be educational, fulfilling, cooperative and satisfying, even if it is hard, as manual labour often is. She envisioned work sites that were small and that allowed workers to see and understand the relationship between their individual effort and the overall process. She also wished to see employees planning their work activities and taking an active role in decisions about production. The division of labour, and the practices of industrialists like Ford and Taylor (inaccurately dubbed 'scientific management'), were anathema to Weil because they increased the atomization of workers, turning them more and more into cogs in a machine. She comments that the treatment of the parts in an assembly line, with each part being labelled, marked for its destination and function, made the parts seems more human than the people, who were treated as anonymous, interchangeable cogs in the industrial machine (Weil, 1951b, p. 247). Describing an organization as a 'machine' came closer to literal description than to metaphor.

Weil's attempts to join the working class were enlightening, if largely unsuccessful. She was no doubt aware that there was a classical precedent in the Greek Stoic philosopher, Cleanthes, who voluntarily took on the mundane task of carrying water. Weil thought that classic Greek literature, philosophy and mythology might make a positive impression on workers and bring about an improvement in their lives, especially because their physical living conditions were similar to physical hardships endured by workers of ancient Greece. Although she saw value in teaching classics to manual labourers, she certainly did *not* disdain physical labour. On the contrary, Weil viewed a labourer's contact with physical reality, with necessity, as a primary way of encountering the world. Indeed, the elevating of manual labour to the same plane as intellectual labour – without devaluing things intellectual – distinguishes Weil's political thought:

> Our age has its own particular mission, or vocation – the creation of a civilization founded upon the spiritual nature of work. The thoughts relating to a presentiment of this vocation, and, which are scattered about in Rousseau, George Sand, Tolstoi, Proudhon, and Marx, in papal encyclicals, and elsewhere, are the only original thoughts of our time, the only ones we haven't borrowed from the Greeks. It is because we have been unequal to this mighty business, which was being conceived in us, that we have thrown ourselves into the abyss presented by totalitarian systems. (Weil, 1952, p. 96)

Reform, revolution and the workers' movement

The brand of Marxism to which Weil was introduced at the Ecole Normale Supérieure owes a debt to Lucien Herr, the librarian there in the late nineteenth century and the teacher of Jean Jaurès during the 1890s. Despite the popularity of Marxism, it was not a sophisticated or a refined philosophy at the point of Weil's introduction to it. The particular brand of Marxist thought that survived tended toward a scientistic, mechanistic materialism, with relatively little attention to traditional philosophical questions. The French understanding of Marxist socialism was also influenced by competing varieties of French revolutionary thought, including Jacobinism, Blanquism, Proudhon's theories, and syndicalism. The early French proponents of Marxist thought, Paul Lafargue and Charles Longuet, so distorted his concepts that Marx claimed 'I am not a Marxist' in response to their interpretation and depiction of his work (in Hirsch, 1981, p. 8). Marx's early works, including the *Paris Manuscripts of 1844*, were not even translated into French until 1937; even then, they were largely ignored until after the Liberation in 1945.

In May 1935, Weil found herself swept up by the euphoria accompanying a series of strikes, and when she visited the factories, she was delighted to find the kind of camaraderie, singing, joking and self-esteem among the workers that she had imagined. She was nevertheless suspicious of *any* mass movement, because she recognized that a heightened 'group sensibility' increased the likelihood of the use of force to achieve group aims. Although she felt sympathy for revolutionary movements, her experience with real workers made her more of a reformist than a revolutionary. Weil had not abandoned her desire to see a fundamental change regarding the role of labour in society, but she also recognized an immediate need for incremental reform:

> So long as such a thing as a society exists, it will circumscribe the life of individuals within quite narrow limits and impose its rules on them; but this inevitable constraint does not merit the name of oppression except in so far as, owing to the fact that it brings about a division between those who exercise it and those who are subject to it, it places the latter at the disposal of the former and thus causes those who command to exert a crushing physical and moral pressure over those who execute. (Weil, 1973, pp. 55–6)

> To imagine that we can switch the course of history along a different track by transforming the system through reforms or revolutions, to hope to find salvation in a defensive or offensive action against tyranny and militarism – all that is just daydreaming. There is nothing on which to base even attempts. . . . The truth is that, to quote a famous saying, slavery degrades man to the point of making him love it; that liberty is precious only in the eyes of those who effectively possess it; and that a completely inhuman system, as ours is, far from producing beings capable of building up a human society, models all those subjected to it – oppressed and oppressors alike – according to its own image.
>
> The only possibility of salvation would lie in a methodical co-operation between all, strong and weak, with a view to accomplishing a progressive decentralization of social life. . . . Such a form of

co-operation is impossible to imagine, even in dreams, in a civilization that is based on competition, on struggle, on war. (Weil, 1973, pp. 116–20)

Everything that contributes towards giving those who are at the bottom of the social scale the feeling that they possess a value is to a certain extent subversive. (Weil, 1973, p. 145)

Weil's assessment of political strategies intended to redress social inequalities calls into question the notion of guaranteed rights *in isolation* and criticizes the foundation of most modern political movements for equality. In the first place, she holds that political ideologies that separate a right from its concomitant obligation are inadequate:

The notion of obligations comes before that of rights, which is subordinate and relative to the former. A right is not effectual by itself, but only in relation to the obligation to which it corresponds. (Weil, 1952, p. 3)

Secondly, political movements that rely on force as a solution to social conditions are inherently tainted, and their insistence on a concept of material progress places them under further suspicion. As an alternative, Weil advances a concept that bridges workers' rights and obligations, by balancing the obsession with productivity with a need for spiritual satisfaction from work. Put another way, we may say that Weil views positively Karl Marx's *diagnosis* of the horrendous conditions in which many people labour – while still rejecting as inadequate much of his prescription:

Marx, who is almost always very strong when he describes simply the bad, has legitimately condemned as a step backwards the separation of manual labor from intellectual work. But he did not know that in all domains contraries (or opposites) have their unity in a transcendent plan, one in relation to the other. The point of unity of intellectual and manual labor is contemplation, which is not work. (Weil, 1951b, p. 270)

Weil argues that both the hope for excessive power or wealth and the fear of want or domination should be eliminated from the workplace. Further, a rigid hierarchical pyramid of authority should be avoided insofar as it is possible to do so – especially where the distribution of power reflects a split between 'manual' labour and 'intellectual' labour. Because smaller workplaces are less likely to require multiple lines of authority – fewer levels of hierarchy – she advances the idea that 'the small peasant property is better than the large. In addition, in all cases where the small is possible, largeness is a bad thing' (Weil, 1951b, p. 272).

Weil recommends that we think not only of avoiding misery for workers, but more importantly, of providing them with joy by way of such activities as a 'tour of France as they used to be done', in order 'to satiate their desire to see and learn' (Weil, 1951b, p. 273). Again, she uses a food metaphor which subordinates physical comforts to spiritual nourishment. She also calls for 'brilliant celebrations' to create the 'supernatural poetry which ought to bathe their entire lives' (Weil, 1951b, p. 273). Unlike the rich English gentleman's Grand Tour of Europe, Weil's tour would foster greater equality and allow factory and field workers to savour the poetry of their surroundings, in much the same way that the upper, leisured classes have done for centuries:

> Equality is a vital need of the human soul. It consists in a recognition, at once public, general, effective, and genuinely expressed in institutions and customs, that the same amount of respect and consideration is due to every human being because this respect is due to the human being as such and is not a matter of degree. . . . Equality is all the greater in proportion as different human conditions are regarded as being, not more nor less than one another, but simply as other. Let us look on the professions of miner and minister simply as two different vocations, like those of poet and mathematician. And let the material hardships attaching to the miner's condition be counted in honor of those who undergo them. (Weil, 1952, pp. 16–18)

Rarely is Weil so effusive or sensual in describing her ideal society as she is when addressing the issue of the proper relationship between people and their work. Her experience as a worker gave her a vision of the possibility of real joy in the workplace and the countryside. Again, Weil envisioned work that was educational, fulfilling and satisfying and that allowed workers to see and understand their own effort as part of a larger scheme. As individual workers gained a proper relationship to their work, so they would become aware of a connection between the necessities of the physical world and the spiritual beauty that accompanies a willing obedience to these physical laws: 'The whole of humanity once lived inspired by the dazzling conception that the universe in which we find ourselves is nothing else than perfect obedience' (Weil, 1952, p. 290). For Weil, physical labour can serve as the 'spiritual core' of an ideal society, because it teaches humanity this perfect obedience; antithetically, 'nothing in the world can make up for the loss of joy in one's work' (Weil, 1952, p. 81). Thus, concludes Weil, 'our age has its own particular mission, or vocation – the creation of a civilization founded upon the spiritual nature of work' (Weil, 1952, p. 96).

John Hellman praises Weil's contribution to labour issues very highly indeed: 'Almost unique in her generation of intellectuals (and our own), she decided to get to know the workers' life firsthand, by sharing it with them, despite the fact that few in her milieu seemed more ill-suited, physically or by family background, for such an initiative' (Hellman, 1982, p. 20). As one of the few highly educated women of her generation to work in fields and factories voluntarily, Weil was uniquely qualified to advise on ways to improve working conditions through physical and educational changes. Her experience and writings on these subjects may have been discounted because of her gender, however, and it may be that any major rethinking of the concept of work could come only decades later, after a sustained feminist critique with a focus on paid labour alone. In a similar vein,

George Abbott White observed that the omission of Weil's work on labour from the English translations constituted a grave loss to reformers in England and the United States:

> The many-million English and American trade unionists were thereby denied an important text, to say nothing of the English-speaking New Left with its resurgent Marxist-Leninist emphasis upon the working class. (White, 1981, p. 185)

In addition to Weil's contributions to the thinking on the political dimensions of labour, she was well ahead of her time in her understanding of cultural issues of identity as it pertains to labour. Her work *The Need for Roots* analyses root causes of racial and class conflicts in industrialized societies; further, her description of the vicious in-fighting, rootlessness and anomie of her own culture anticipates the postmodern condition of the latter half of the twentieth century.

Thoughts on politics: the role of the state

Simone Weil's discussion of political issues ranges across a number of apparently disparate topics, including technology, trade unions, sexual practices, regional history, worldwide colonialism, and ethics. Her political consciousness is inextricably bound with the empathy and respect she holds for the dignity of common people, particularly those on the fringes of society. Thus, she focuses on ethical and practical suggestions essential for altering a society that has been fabricated from injustice, inequality and degradation:

> Deprivation of honor attains its extreme degree with that total deprivation of respect reserved for certain categories of human beings. In France, this affects under various forms, prostitutes, ex-convicts, police agents, and the subproletariat composed of colonial immigrants and natives. Categories of this kind ought not to exist. (Weil, 1952, p. 20)

What is the use of workmen obtaining as a result of their struggles an increase in wages and a relaxation of discipline, if meanwhile engineers in a few research departments invent, without the slightest evil intent, machines which reduce their souls and bodies to a state of exhaustion, or aggravate their economic difficulties . . . . Even Soviet propaganda has never claimed that Russia had discovered a radically new type of machine, worthy of being handled by an all-powerful proletariat. And yet, if there is one conviction which stands out with irresistible force in the works of Marx, it is this one: that any change in the relationship between the classes must remain a pure illusion, if it be not accompanied by a transformation in technical processes, expressing itself in entirely new types of machinery. (Weil, 1952, p. 57)

Weil recommends three qualities that a transformation in technical processes should possess. The first is that it should not cause exhaustion or accidental physical harm to the user. The second characteristic concerns the flexibility of machines: they should be adaptable to multiple purposes. The third is that the machine should be something that an ordinary person can operate.

Weil envisions a society in which relatively small collectives produce a certain number of items, with work groups determining the best ways of achieving that end. Spouses and children might come home after school, visit the workplace, and even assist in production. Weil relatedly argues that the state must assume the responsibility for apprenticeship, and that without this training a society is economically bankrupt and ill prepared for military emergencies. She notes that

even in 1934 and 1935, when the unemployment crisis had reached its height, when production was at a dead point, engineering and aviation works were looking for good professional workmen and couldn't find them. The workmen complained that the tests were too difficult; but it was they who hadn't received the necessary training so as to be able to carry out the tests. (Weil, 1952, p. 62)

When Weil argues for training workers and for work apprenticeships, she is *not* advocating a narrow type of technical or industrial education for workers, devoid of intellectual content. Rather, she advocates educating workers in a broad sense of the term – even teaching the classics – so that a society has a deep pool of educated, trained, experienced and 'cultured' individuals. The problem, continues Weil, is that current ways of conveying culture ('teaching') are often inadequate to the task, because the material is conveyed in a manner that renders it irrelevant and inaccessible to most people:

> Culture – as we know it – is an instrument manipulated by teachers for manufacturing more teachers, who, in turn, will manufacture still more teachers. (Weil, 1952, p. 68)

Where classical sources ('culture') have been transformed into textbooks, the results have all too often been mutilated, with little connection either to real-life experience or to the passion that animated the original work. By counter-example, Weil suggests teaching geometry by having students build objects that demonstrate specific mathematical principles. Her technique is remarkably similar to the current practice of using 'manipulatable' objects to teach children mathematics, but it is even more thoroughly grounded in the social reality of the world of work. Similarly, Weil argues that literature must be taught in ways that show the connection between fictional characters' experiences and the living realities of ordinary readers: 'A workman, for instance, who bears the anguish of unemployment deep in the very marrow of his bones, would understand the feelings of Philoctetus when his bow is taken away from him, and the despair with which he stares at his powerless hands' (Weil, 1952, p. 70).

For Weil, the transmission of culture is a fundamental responsibility of the state, one which should be wedded to the promoting of rootedness in those who work the land. Workers who are disenfranchised and alienated in the modern workplace may be as emotionally and spiritually damaged as the peasants of feudal societies. Any political, state or social institution that reduces the esteem of workers or weakens their connection to spiritual values thereby weakens the fabric of society. As an antidote to institutions that 'uproot' individuals, Weil postulates a society founded on the 'spirituality of work':

> The word spirituality doesn't imply any particular affiliation. Even the Communists, in the present state of things, would probably not reject it. Besides, it would not be difficult to find in Marx quotations that can all be brought back to the reproach of lack of spirituality leveled at capitalist society; which implies that there ought to be some in the new society. The conservative parties wouldn't dare to reject such a conception; nor would radical, laical, or masonic circles either. Christians would seize on it with joy. It would create unanimity. (Weil, 1952, p. 97)

Just as Weil balances rights with obligations, so she addresses not only the role of social institutions, but also the responsibility of individuals to the state. In speaking about patriotism, her analysis is subtle and complex. She argues that the state of mind that we signify via the word 'patriotism' once existed as 'something diffuse, nomadic, which expanded or contracted according to degrees of similarity and common danger. It was mixed up with different kinds of loyalty – loyalty to other men, a lord, a king, or a city', and it pre-dates the nation state by centuries (Weil, 1952, p. 104). Then, tracing the history of French nationalism, Weil questions the shifting nature of the concept of 'nation'. She notes the frequent shifting of allegiances, with France often being ruled by English kings, and isolated regions of the country often resisting domination by the reigning French monarch. Weil concludes that the notion of loyalty to the state, of patriotism, first appears in the seventeenth century with Richelieu, and that this historical period marks the beginning of a totalitarian mindset – a focus on present needs and future goals of the ruler and a blatant (and intentional) disregard of the past. It is this condition that Weil identifies as uprootedness: a loss of any sense of the past and of respect for tradition; a forced obedience to the current regime, rather than loyalty or devotion to legitimate authority; and a state of helplessness and alienation instilled in the masses, rather than voluntary participation in public life or commitment to the society:

> To be rooted is perhaps the most important and least recognized need of the human soul. (Weil, 1952, p. 43)

> Uprootedness is by far the most dangerous malady to which human societies are exposed, for it is a self-propagating one. For people who are really uprooted there remain only two possible sorts of behavior: either to fall into a spiritual lethargy resembling death, like the majority of slaves in the days of the Roman Empire, or to hurl themselves into some form of activity necessarily designed to uproot, often by the most violent methods, those who are not yet uprooted, or only partly so. (Weil, 1952, p. 47)

> But with morals, properly speaking, thus relegated to a lower plane, no other system is advanced as a substitute. For the superior prestige of the nation is bound up with the exaltation of war. It furnishes no motives for action in peacetime, except in a regime which constitutes a permanent preparation for war, like the Nazi regime. (Weil, 1952, p. 139)

> Thus we have witnessed this strange spectacle – a State, the object of hatred, repugnance, derision, disdain, and fear, which under the name of *patrie*, demanded absolute loyalty, total self-abnegation, the supreme sacrifice, and obtained them, from 1914 to 1918, to an extent which surpassed all expectations. (Weil, 1952, p. 128)

> The very word politics had taken on a profoundly pejorative meaning. . . . 'Oh, he's a politician,' 'All that, that's just politics' – such phrases expressed final and complete condemnation. (Weil, 1952, p. 121)

Because people who are uprooted still have a need to belong, a need to extend the perimeters of self, they are also vulnerable to manipulation of charismatic leaders with a 'cause' and to manipulation by the media; moreover, individuals who are already uprooted are more susceptible to 'blind' devotion:

Just now, there is in all countries, in all movements, a man who is the personal magnet for all loyalties. Being compelled to embrace the cold, metallic surface of the State has made people, by contrast, hunger for something to love which is made of flesh and blood. This phenomenon shows no signs of disappearing, and however disastrous the consequences have been so far, it may still have some very unpleasant surprises in store for us; for the art, so well known in Hollywood, of manufacturing stars out of any sort of human material, gives any sort of person the opportunity of presenting himself for the adoration of the masses. (Weil, 1952, pp. 114–15)

People who are uprooted may take yet another tack: they may personify the state and then fanatically pledge their allegiance to it regardless of morality: 'My country, right or wrong.' Weil notes how a number of actions that would be unconscionable or, at the very least, in bad taste, in one's personal life are not only acceptable but obligatory behaviour for nations: boasting, ignoring the needs and rights of others, reminding others of all the favours one has done them, and so on. As an example, she cites an irony that she perceives in France's patriotic resistance to the Germans, at least when juxtaposed to its own imperialistic forays:

The good people who talked thus had a general idea of the history of France, but they didn't pause to think, when they were speaking, that the national unity had been brought about almost exclusively by the most brutal conquests. . . . Is it not just as easy to be ignorant of the cruelties of the Germans toward the Jews or the Czechs as it is of those of the French toward the Annamites? (Weil, 1952, p. 145).

Whereas pride in national glory is by its nature exclusive, non-transferable, compassion is by its nature universal; it is only more potential where distant and unfamiliar things are concerned, more real, more physical, or charged with blood, tears, and effective energy where things close at hand are concerned. (Weil, 1952, p. 174).

In *The Need for Roots*, Weil outlines problems likely to face France following the end of World War II and what she perceives

as the inevitable defeat of Germany. She first considers how
leaders can inspire a nation to proper action, but finds that no
clear examples exist to achieve such an ideal goal. Weil next
looks to education, but quickly dismisses the most common
modes of motivation employed in that context: threats,
promises and suggestions. What Weil then envisions is that a
dialogue should be established, facilitated by a network of
people who talk with and listen to the people of France. To 're-
root' a society of uprooted individuals through such a dialogue
is to set off on a quest – educational, vocational, political and
spiritual. Further, this quest must engage individuals on the
basis of intrinsic merits, and it must not resort to means
inevitably employed by the state, namely, coercion and force:

> The true mission of the French movement in London is, by reason
> even of the military and political circumstances, a spiritual mission
> before being a military and political one. (Weil, 1952, p. 215)

> But why should politics, which decide the fate of peoples and whose
> object is justice, demand any less concentration than art or science,
> whose respective objects are beauty and truth?
>   Politics have a very close affinity to art – to arts such as poetry,
> music, and architecture. (Weil, 1952, p. 216)

> Politics, in their turn, form an art governed by composition on a
> multiple plane. Whoever finds himself with political responsibilities,
> if in his heart he hungers and thirsts after justice, must desire to
> possess this faculty of composition on a multiple plane, and conse-
> quently is bound, in the end, to receive it. (Weil, 1952, p. 217)

> Four obstacles above all separate us from a form of civilization likely
> to be worth something: our false conception of greatness; the degra-
> dation of the sentiment of justice; our idolization of money; and our
> lack of religious inspiration. . . .
>   Our conception of greatness is the very one that has inspired
> Hitler's whole life. When we denounce it without the remotest
> recognition of its application to ourselves, the angels must either cry
> or laugh, if there happen to be angels who interest themselves in
> our propaganda. (Weil, 1952, p. 219)

No attention is paid to the defeated. It is the scene of a Darwinian process more pitiless still than that which governs animal and vegetable life. The defeated disappear. They become naught. (Weil, 1952, p. 222)

In order to love France, we must feel that she has a past; but we must not love the historical wrapper of that past. We must love the part that is inarticulate, anonymous, which has vanished. (Weil, 1952, p. 232)

Assessing Weil's political thought

In assessing Weil's political thinking, it is important to avoid the clichés and labels that constitute much political discourse. Attempting to orient her thought along a single continuum, whether identified as liberal–conservative, left–right, or status quo–radical, is as tempting as it is simplistic. Weil herself insisted that such labels obscure understanding rather than increase it: 'They content themselves with uttering a few eulogistic epithets . . . . They haven't tired themselves' (Weil, 1978, pp. 1–2). Weil believed that the use of simplistic labels, often little more than clichés, obscures perceptions of reality.

A more useful way of understanding Weil's ideas about politics is by reference to what she sees as the errors of past and existing political groupings. While she agrees with Marx's critique regarding the need to value manual labour, she recognizes that such a manoeuvre should not involve devaluing the intellect. To do so, asserts Weil, is simply to substitute one form of tyranny for another. Although she supports attempts by workers to resist conditions of oppression, she notes that at one point the Communist Party was even prepared to support the Hitlerite movement. Thus, argues Weil, the Communists succeeded in 'perfecting' the machinery of the state instead of 'destroying' it (Weil, 1987, p. 141).

That the workers in the factories are resisting Hitlerite demagogy proves that, in spite of the miserable situation to which they have been reduced – their low wages, the lack of job security, the factory shutdowns that shorten their working hours and affect their whole family – they are not giving way to despair. One cannot admire them enough. (Weil, 1987, p. 119)

The Hitlerites actually began to murder Communists in their homes or in the streets; there was a whole series of bloody skirmishes between Hitlerites and Communists. From that time on the Communist party was forced, despite the resolutions of the Eleventh Plenum, to reverse its position and direct its efforts mainly against fascism. (Weil, 1987, p. 129)

As for the trade-union funds, their very wealth makes them dependent on the state, the protector of capital. (Weil, 1987, p. 110)

Even should there come a stage of the capitalist economy in which Marx's formula is proved to be true, in which the regime deprives the workers of everything except their chains, it would not be possible for the German trade unions to change the purpose for which they were originally intended and become instruments suitable for overthrowing the regime; any more than a file, in case of need, could change itself into a hammer. (Weil, 1987, p. 111)

It is the *means* of the state, regardless of political end, that most troubles Weil. Indeed, social institutions, be they government, church or trade union, may resort to using a means that works against their stated ends. The reliance of the state on power and force, for example, militates against conditions necessary for rootedness – regardless of political ideology. Whereas other scholars and observers may evaluate a political entity simply according to ideology – communist is 'bad', Fascist is 'good', and so on – Weil perceives the matter as much more complex. She realized that even the Christian Church, existing within a 'democratic' society, could uproot its members. To understand Weil's political thinking more fully, one must place it alongside her thoughts on aggression and oppression.

Aggression and Oppression
Suffering Selves

In considering the life and work of Simone Weil, her interpreters have found few points of agreement. An apparent exception lies in the assessment of her thoughts and actions as they relate to war, force and aggression. Her devotion to a position of pacifism is quite clear and her eventual acceptance of the necessity to take a stand against the Fascist juggernaut rolling over Europe is part and parcel of her steadfast opposition to force. In an eloquent and powerful statement, Weil declares that 'where force is absolutely sovereign, justice is absolutely unreal' (Weil, 1952, p. 243).

Aggression and the reliance on force

It is a commonplace to say that we should learn from the past. While a number of people talk about learning lessons from history, Weil actually did so, matching and contrasting the situations of the Romanization of ancient Greece with Hitler's takeover of Europe. Framing her discussion in terms of a time-less Manichaean struggle between forces of good and evil, she examines figures and movements throughout history and across the globe to determine when and where moments of illumination occurred, and how these flashes were then extin-guished by aggression and violence. She goes back to the twelfth- and thirteenth-century crusade against the Cathars, for example, to illustrate how Western civilization rejected an opportunity to follow a genuine Christian path, and she com-pares this early case of oppression with the events that surrounded her in Europe.

Like many subsequent feminist theorists, Weil was con-cerned about the untold story of those silenced by oppression. Mark Taylor observes that Weil, 'as a social activist, as educa-tional theorist, and as philosopher of history . . . championed those passive victims whose goodness history had rewarded with silence. Hers was a defeated, anonymous and vanished constituency: those peoples, simply, who had lost, as they nearly always would in this world, and whose losing meant neglect or calumny in the official chronicles of their conquerors.' An exam-ple of the people Weil admired were the Cathars, whom Charles Homer Haskins notes were only described in the writings of their enemies (Taylor, in Haskins, 1927, p. 451).

Throughout the corpus of her work, Weil's intricate under-standing of aggression brings to mind the visual image of a spiral. Each time an individual is dealt a blow by another human being, a disturbance in the equilibrium occurs; this disturbance must inevitably energize a response by the victim. When one responds with force against another person – even if it is not against the original aggressor – then the cycle of overt aggres-sion is passed on. Both the aggressor and the victim experience force; thus, everyone who is subjected to the contact of force is defiled – whether aggressor or target of aggression (Weil, 1957, p. 24ff.):

Everything that is subjected to the contact of force is defiled, whatever the contact. To strike or to be struck is one and the same defilement. The chill of steel is equally mortal at the hilt and at the point. (Weil, 1962, p. 49)

Human history is simply the history of the servitude which makes men – oppressors and oppressed alike – the plaything of the instruments of domination they themselves have manufactured, and thus reduces living humanity to being the chattel of inanimate chattels. (Weil, 1973, p. 69)

Such is the nature of might. Its power to transform man into a thing is double and it cuts both ways; it petrifies differently but equally the souls of those who suffer it, and of those who wield it. (Weil, 1957, pp. 44–5)

Should one refuse to direct that force outward, then the force takes its toll within the boundaries of the self, a toll that may manifest itself either as oppression (literally, 'to press down') or depression (literally, 'to be pressed down'). Either way, the movement represents a downward spiral; the common destiny of humanity descends an ever-widening path of destruction.

Weil perceives the transition from Greek to Roman civilization as an example here. Her strong aversion to Roman civilization, especially in contrast to her praise of ancient Greek thought, hinges primarily on her reading of ancient Rome as a culture that glorified force, might and war. While Weil is quite ready to declare it a right, even a duty, to defend life, liberty and roots (or country), she perceived that much of war has had little to do with noble aims. Instead, 'when men are offered the choice between guns and butter, although they prefer butter so very much more than guns, a mysterious fatality compels them, in spite of themselves, to choose guns' (Weil, 1952, p. 96). It is this 'mysterious fatality' that Weil laments and that she believes is partially attributable to the false glorification of force, and partially to the cycle of violence – using force against others in response to prior aggressions against oneself.

Any social group founded on force prompted Weil's criticism, and the nearer her roots to such a society, the more intense was her reaction. Such is the case with Weil's criticisms of Judaism. What previous commentators have failed to perceive, however, are elements of her thought that actually converge with Judaism. Weil criticizes Martin Buber's concept of the élan in Hasidic thought, but she shares his views on relatedness. Buber (1952, 1970) took great care to distinguish between 'I–Thou' relationships, which affirm and extend each person's humanity as they transact or interact, and 'I–It' relationships, wherein one person is reduced to the level of object. The former, according to Buber, are animated by *hesed*, by love, while the latter are driven by force. Weil's statements parallel this distinction:

> Might is that which makes a thing of anybody who comes under its sway. When exercised to the full, it makes a thing of man in the most literal sense, for it makes him a corpse. There where someone stood a moment ago, stands no one. (Weil, 1957, p. 24)

> From the power to transform man into a thing by killing him there proceeds another power, and much more prodigious, that which makes a thing of him while he still lives. He is living, he has a soul, yet he is a thing. (Weil, 1957, p. 26)

> The supernatural virtue of justice consists of behaving exactly as though there were equality when one is the stronger in an unequal relationship. (Weil, 1951a, p. 143)

> 'YOU do not interest me.' No man can say these words to another without committing a cruelty and offending against justice. (Weil, 1981, p. 13)

Aggression and academia

It is relatively easy to make statements against aggression and compose pithy essays decrying oppressive conditions within a society. What makes Weil's approach so different from those of other theorists is her willingness to go beyond making statements and enter into a steadfast commitment of congruency between thought and action. For example, Weil's rejection of violence led her to protest against protection of the civilian population during warfare. Her logic was that the likelihood of war increases by ensuring the safety of the government, military staff and civilians. Conversely, when every member of society is placed in harm's way, people's eagerness to participate in warfare decreases. Some critics condemn Weil's activities in the war and her employment as a factory worker. Yet these activities, interpreted in terms of her commitment to a harmony of thought and action, crystallize as principled behaviour performed 'without regard for results'. In contrast to Weil's example, the collective response of academics to Fascism during the 1930s and early 1940s appears unprincipled and cowardly. Köhler, a German psychologist who wrote the last anti-Nazi piece published in Germany, commented on the academic response to Nazism:

> Nothing astonished the Nazis so much as the cowardice of whole university faculties, which did not consist of Nazis. Naturally this corroborated the Nazis' contempt for the intellectual life. (Köhler in Henle, 1978, p. 940)

Academic critics who belittle Weil's thought or efforts may in fact be threatened by her example. What would it be like to live life on Weil's terms? For one thing, such a person could no longer cling to the belief that thinking about and writing about an issue are synonymous with enacting a solution to it. It is certainly easier to criticize Weil's example than to take such a challenging and risky stance in life. While the lives of many academics are lived cautiously and narrowly, Weil's sense of vocation and her courage demanded engagement in the world outside of those intellectual confines: 'But words are only a beginning. Action is a more powerful tool for molding people's minds' (Weil, 1952, p. 203).

A related basis for criticizing Weil's writings against the use of force arises from territorialism in academic disciplines. Weil's work here ranges over a number of fields, from her literary criticism of the *Iliad* to her suggestions for battlefield resistance tactics, from thoughts on education to religion, and from philosophy to economics; consequently, she has incurred the wrath of many specialists who wish to quibble with her statements within 'their' field of expertise. Ferber and Summers (in White, 1981), for example, criticize her 'partial readings' of the *Iliad*, even taking her to task over the proper translation of the Greek word for 'gently' (Greek: *eka*). Devotees of specialization are right in recognizing an enemy in Weil, for her answers to the problems of aggression and oppression reside in a broad education – one that requires students to grapple with a number of intellectual disciplines. The main purpose of education, as Weil sees it, is not to become expert in some limited domain, but to apply education – regardless of discipline – to the search for truth and to develop in students the capacity for attention. These emphases reflect Weil's intellectual commitment:

> It is true that men are capable of dividing their minds into compartments, in each of which an idea lives a sort of life of its own, undisturbed by other ideas. They don't care for either critical or synthetic effort, and won't submit to making either unless obliged. (Weil, 1952, pp. 134–5)

It is no surprise, then, that Weil calls for an educational system that places moral inquiry at its centre and for a government that entrusts political power only to those citizens who have been broadly educated. To fail to do so, Weil contends, is to place political power in the hands of individuals who rely on force, rather than reason. To fail to do so is to set up conditions likely to result in oppression:

> What conclusion is there to be drawn other than that morals are among the number of less important things, which, like religion, a

trade, the choice of a doctor or a grocer, belong to the lower plane of private life? (Weil, 1952, p. 139)

The soul of a child, as it reaches out toward understanding, has need of the treasures accumulated by the human species through the centuries. (Weil, 1952, pp. 91–2)

Education – whether its object be children or adults, individuals or an entire people, or even oneself – consists in creating motives. To show what is beneficial, what is obligatory, what is good – that is the task of education. Education concerns itself with the motives for effective action. For no action is ever carried out in the absence of motives capable of supplying the indispensable amount of energy for its execution. (Weil, 1952, pp. 189–90)

To want to direct human creatures – others or oneself – toward the good by simply pointing out the direction, without making sure the necessary motives have been provided, is as if one tried, by pressing down the accelerator, to set off in a motorcar with an empty gas tank. (Weil, 1952, p. 190)

Academic work is one of those fields containing a pearl so precious that it is worthwhile to sell all our possessions, keeping nothing for ourselves, in order to be able to acquire it. (Weil, 1951a, p. 116)

Aggression and oppression: suffering selves

Given the world as it is, rather than as it ought to be, Weil scrutinizes the relationship between social oppression and personal suffering. Simone Weil's abhorrence of violence and aggression extends to any sort of oppression occurring in the world, including slavery and political subjugation. She makes a distinction, however, between suffering, which may actually produce some enlightenment, and affliction, which crushes the spirit through simultaneous physical, mental and social torment. Affliction crushes individuals and renders their hearts mute; it delivers its shock in full magnitude through the spirit of each individual. For Weil, the blows of aggression never lose their power to wound the individual soul.

Whereas most of Weil's contemporaries attributed political abuses to particular ideologies, Weil probed deeper for the sources of oppression. She identified its contributing causes as everything from the worship of science (Chapter 1), the role of the individual within a collective (Chapter 2), and the failure of attention (Chapter 3) to the status of manual labour and society's ordering of political values (Chapter 4). And just as she described affliction as affecting every segment of society, from 'top' to 'bottom', Weil extended the notion of culpability to include every level; she perceived all of us as accomplices to affliction. During the Spanish Civil War, for instance, Weil confessed that she had wished for the defeat of Franco's forces, and that she was therefore 'morally an accomplice' in the spilling of blood (McFarland, 1983, p. 81). For Simone Weil, 'any blow we suffer, whether in the form of a pain or an insult, is automatically communicated to some person or object outside us in a sense as material as the transfer of force in the action and reaction of atoms' (Taubes, 1955, p. 8). We 'pass on' blows that we have experienced ('passed through'):

> When we hit a nail with a hammer, the whole of the shock received by the large head of the nail passes into the point without any of it being lost, although it is only a point. If the hammer and the head of the nail were infinitely big it would be just the same. The point of the nail would transmit this infinite shock at the point to which it was applied.
>
> Extreme affliction, which means physical pain, distress of soul, and social degradation, all at the same time, is a nail whose point is applied at the very center of the soul, whose head is all necessity spreading throughout space and time. (Weil, 1951a, pp. 134–5)

In the realm of suffering, affliction is something apart, specific, and irreducible. It is quite a different thing from simple suffering. It takes possession of the soul and marks it through and through with its own particular mark, the mark of slavery. Slavery as practiced by ancient Rome is only an extreme form of affliction. The men of antiquity, who knew all about this question, used to say: 'A man loses half his soul the day he becomes a slave.' (Weil, 1951a, p. 117)

In those who have suffered too many blows, in slaves for example, that place in the heart from which the infliction of evil evokes a cry of surprise may seem to be dead. But it is never quite dead; it is simply unable to cry out any more. It has sunk into a state of dumb and ceaseless lamentation. (Weil, 1962, p. 11)

Although it may seem facile to assert that one who thinks about another person's pain experiences the same pain, in the case of Simone Weil, this may have been in some sense true. To the extent that an individual opens up to the affliction of others, the individual *passes* the experience *through* her consciousness; she experiences the event. If an event has not passed through her consciousness, she has not in any sense experienced the affliction. The connection between 'passing through' and suffering is even more intricate and complex, however. Implicit in Weil's understanding is the possibility that someone hearing of another's affliction suffers the experience more acutely than those observers living in the midst of another's affliction. Counter-intuitive as it seems, two important principles account for this paradox. First, a person in the midst of suffering can at least make some effort to alleviate the problems of others – even if only for one person or one day, through one generous act. In contrast, to know of another's affliction and to feel so removed from the event that one is helpless to intervene can accentuate one's suffering. Secondly, a person living in the midst of some human disaster or chronic social problem may not experience the event as acutely as a person more distant from it because of what perception theorists call *sensory adaptation*, that is, a natural tendency to cease paying attention to events that are unchanging. In this context, the concept suggests that people living amidst a chronic condition become desensitized to the plight of their immediate 'neighbours'.

Taken together, these two principles may help explain the expression of intense struggle and profound suffering that one encounters in Weil's work. Critics and sceptics frequently point to the fact that Weil *chose* to suffer physical hardships, and that this evidence *diminishes* the authenticity of her experience: she only visited rather than inhabited the world of poverty. This criticism in fact completely misses the point, which is that Weil denied herself food and other comforts *precisely because* she had the luxury of doing so. No doubt, if starvation had been forced upon her, she would have scrambled for every morsel she could find – provided she knew of no one else in worse need than herself. Weil's view is, once again, an incredibly demanding one: to accept the mantle of privilege, while surrounded by persons with no such choice, is to participate in the structure of oppression.

In accordance with her commitment to attention as a method for seeking truth, Weil deliberately passed through a wide range of social conditions: hunger, inequality, force and aggression paramount among them. In response to such conditions, her much-criticized attempts to work in a factory or help out at a battlefront are best viewed as principled efforts to link thought with action. At the same time, Weil's almost frenetic actions to change the world may also be interpreted as attempts to lessen her own suffering. What can otherwise seem erratic actions appear planned and patterned within her ideal of a life devoted to alleviating suffering and affliction:

> Human thought is unable to acknowledge the reality of affliction. To acknowledge the reality of affliction means saying to oneself: 'I may lose at any moment, through the play of circumstances over which I have no control, anything whatsoever that I possess, including those things which are so intimately mine that I consider them as being myself. There is nothing that I might not lose. It could happen at any moment that what I am might be abolished and replaced by anything whatsoever of the filthiest and most contemptible sort.'
>
> To be aware of this in the depth of one's soul is to experience non-being. It is the state of extreme and total humiliation which is also

the condition for passing over into truth. It is a death of the soul. This is why the naked spectacle of affliction makes the soul shudder as the flesh shudders at the proximity of death. (Weil, 1977, p. 332)

For to know, not abstractly but with the whole soul, that all in nature, including psychological nature, is under the dominance of a force as brutal, as pitilessly directed downward as gravity, such a knowledge glues, so to speak, the soul to prayer like a prisoner who, when he is able, remains glued to the window of his cell, or like a fly stays stuck to the bottom of a bottle by the force of its urge toward the light. (Weil, 1957, p. 116)

Given her commitment to a harmonious relation between thought and action, Weil asserts that the way of attention is immeasurably superior to viewing the world through a tinted lens. By attending to the negative aspects of existence and then following those perceptions with actions intended to alleviate them, human beings can create a more egalitarian society. Weil convincingly argues that the world as it is need not be a 'brute given'. She moves intentionally and convincingly from stating 'such *is* the world' to declaring that 'such have we *made* the world'. Far from being a pessimist, Weil states that 'the mere fact that we exist, that we conceive and want something different from what exists, constitutes for us a reason for hoping' (Weil, 1973, pp. 22–3).

Evil and Good

A Move Toward God

Throughout her writings, Simone Weil concerns herself with the problem of evil; her concern increases as she begins to move from an explicitly atheistic position to one of spiritual affirmation. Weil sees discomfort with and revulsion from evil as a motor force driving human beings to a higher plane of thought and understanding:

> We do not ask God to lead us into good, but to deliver us from evil. (Weil, 1956, p. 418)

> In every soul the cry to be delivered from evil is incessant. (Weil, 1962, p. 30)

> There isn't a man on earth who doesn't at times pronounce an opinion on good and evil, even if it be only to find fault with somebody else. (Weil, 1952, p. 158)

> There is no ground for believing that morality has ever changed. There is every ground for believing that men in the most remote ages conceived the good, when they conceived it at all, with the same purity and perfection as ourselves, in spite of the fact that

they practised evil, and praised it when it was victorious, exactly as we do. (Weil, 1962, p. 131)

All Greek civilization is a search for bridges to relate human misery and divine perfection. (Weil, 1957, p. 75)

[A]n act of cruelty in the tenth century is exactly as cruel, neither more nor less so, than an act of cruelty in the nineteenth. (Weil, 1952, p. 229)

Supernatural good is not a sort of supplement to natural good, as we are told, with support from Aristotle, for our greater comfort. It would be nice if this were true, but it is not. In all the crucial problems of human existence the only choice is between supernatural good on the one hand and evil on the other. (Weil, 1962, p. 23)

Weil has little trouble in identifying potential sources of the 'bad', including ignorance, mental laziness, desire for instant gratification, lack of self-discipline, improper social training and a drive for retribution (the vicious cycle of aggression described in the previous chapter). After years of grappling with the question of the 'good', however, Weil can find no rational explanation for the 'good', nor any rational explanation for the source of good thoughts and good behaviours. Indeed, kindness or goodness, according to Weil, is illogical; it is as contradictory as evil:

It is not in the least true that good is without its contradictory side, that evil alone is contradictory. Virtue might well be, perhaps, less logical than sin. (Weil, 1956, p. 4)

There is a reality outside the world, that is to say, outside space and time, outside man's mental universe, outside any sphere whatsoever that is accessible to human faculties. Corresponding to this reality, at the centre of the human heart, is the longing for an absolute good, a longing which is always there and is never appeased by any object in this world. (Weil, 1962, p. 219)

Whoever is capable of a movement of pure compassion towards a person in affliction (a very rare thing anyway) possesses, maybe implicitly, yet always really, the love of God and faith. (Weil, 1953, p. 36)

Religious thought is genuine whenever it is universal in its appeal. (1952, p. 93)

Why give one's heart to anything other than the good? (Weil, 1952, p. 235)

Weil concludes that only something outside the domain of natural processes can account for the good – whether it be the origination of a good thought (like many ideas of ancient Greece), a good feeling (such as compassion for the afflicted), or a good action (such as acting to alleviate suffering of the afflicted). In short, she perceives a *bipolar* structure to reality (material and non-material), to valuation (good and evil), and to one's self: 'I am always double: on one hand, the passive being who is subjected to the world, and on the other, the active being who has a grip on it' (quoted in Pétrement, 1976, p. 66). Just as Descartes moved from *Cogito, ergo sum* (I think, therefore I am) to the existence of innate ideas (including the idea of God), Weil progresses from a perception of 'doubleness' to self to a conclusion that 'self cannot be all that there is':

If nothing but me exists, nothing exists except this absolute power [to decide and to act]. I depend on nothing but my will, I do not exist except insofar as I create myself, I am God. . . . But it's not so. I am not God. Although this power that I possess is by nature infinite, it has some limitations that I must recognize. . . . Therefore, something other than myself exists. (Weil, in Pétrement, 1976, p. 64)

As Weil consciously reaches this understanding that 'something besides myself' must exist, her thought moves progressively toward the language of theology, with the concepts of grace and gravity predominating. By grace, Weil means a principle that accounts for 'the beginning of a thought', something self cannot do or it would then be 'sufficient unto itself';

she confirms that self cannot be 'all there is'. By gravity, Weil means a principle that accounts for the force which 'blindly acts upon self'. The blind action of forces symbolized by her concept of gravity may appear as 'evil' from a limited perspective, but this perception is flawed because it confuses natural consequences with intent. If a young child drowns in the ocean, having been knocked over by a powerful wave, does this incident mean the waves are evil? On the contrary, these waves may be seen as neutral, good or beautiful, even when they result in an outcome that we perceive negatively:

> In the beauty of the world brute necessity becomes an object of love. What is more beautiful than the action of gravity on the fugitive folds of the sea waves, or on the almost eternal folds of the mountains?
> The sea is not less beautiful in our eyes because we know that sometimes ships are wrecked by it. On the contrary, this adds to its beauty. . . .
> All the horrors produced in this world are like the folds imposed upon the waves by gravity. That is why they contain an element of beauty. (Weil, 1951a, pp. 128–9)

> God does not send sufferings and woes as ordeals; he lets Necessity distribute them in accordance with its own proper mechanism. (Weil, 1970, p. 403)

> This world, insofar as it is quite empty of God, is God himself. Necessity insofar as it is absolutely distinct from goodness, is goodness itself. . . . Therein lies the mystery of mysteries. (Weil, 1963, p. xxv)

While Weil uses the concepts of grace and gravity as her thought moves more decidedly in a religious direction, there is nothing accidental or discontinuous in this move. When speaking in her more philosophical voice, Weil struggles with the apparent duality of the universe and conveys the bipolarity in terms of freedom versus necessity. In surveying Weil's thought, one sees that the pattern is clearly of a piece. The following quotation, for instance, is as consistent with 'early' Weil as it is with Weil in the last years of her life:

> [The world is ruled by necessity, a] blind mechanism [which] . . . continually tosses men about . . .
>
> If the mechanism were not blind there would not be any affliction. Affliction is anonymous before all things; it deprives its victims of their personality and makes them into things. It is indifferent; and it is the coldness of this indifference – a metallic coldness – that freezes all those it touches right to the depths of their souls. . . .
>
> Affliction would not have this power without the element of chance contained by it. (1951a, pp. 124–5)

A survey of Weil's thought quickly unveils her desire to achieve a resolution of apparent duality, of polarities, many of which are not the usual contraries or antinomies with which philosophers have traditionally concerned themselves. A great deal of her thought, for instance, is structured around an inherent tension between *interconnected* opposing entities: force/love, self/world, freedom/necessity, providence/chance, grace/gravity, and God/world. The polarities differ depending on the plane on which Simone Weil is speaking (social, physical, philosophical, political or religious), but the congruence between them is quite clear. Even Weil's approach to method reflects this bipolar structure. Attention can now be more clearly understood: the capacity for attention is difficult because a person must maintain 'a tension between opposing tendencies'. To refuse to close the gap prematurely, to remain intentionally in this state of perceptual openness, is not unlike being hungry yet refusing to eat. At the very core of Weil's life and work, a key to the mystery of her life and her death, is her perception of life as equivalent to being hungry yet refusing to eat, that is, as a polarity of looking (attending, without closure) versus eating (consuming, with immediate closure).

The choice not to eat in the face of hunger constitutes one of the most important threads of Weil's life. From the very earliest months of infancy through to her death, she chose to deny herself food even when hungry. The act of eating is not restricted to the physical plane, however. In speaking about intellectual progress, Weil remarked that 'I only read what I am hungry for at the moment when I have an appetite for it, and then I do not read, I eat' (Weil, 1951a, p. 69). When her thought becomes more spiritual in content, she frames this metamorphosis with the metaphorical language of food and eating. As Weil noted, it was during the recitation of George Herbert's poem 'Love' that she had her first religious experience. The last four lines of the poem convey the essence of Weil's quest for spiritual satisfaction and embody this quest in the metaphor of eating:

> 'And know you not,' says Love, 'Who bore the blame?'
>   'My dear, then I will serve.'
> 'You must sit down,' says Love, 'and taste my meat.'
>   So I did sit and eat.

7

The Mystical Moment
An Affirmation of God

Weil's 'mystical moment'

The moment of mystical union, wherein Weil declared that 'Christ himself came down and took possession' of her, provides a precise point for mapping her religious journey. According to Robert Coles, 'this event took place in 1938 or 1939, as she approached thirty', although before that she had 'three contacts with Catholicism that really counted' (Coles, 1987, p. 114). Even though some interest in spiritual matters surfaced throughout her life, this moment represents a dramatic movement from her explicit atheism during the time she was teaching (1931–33). The mystical moment here was intense and life-changing. Her mystical experience bears resemblance to that of other renowned mystics such as Teresa of Avila, Catherine of Siena, Meister Eckhardt and Hildegard of Bingen, although Weil defined her experience in reference to the Cathars of twelfth- and thirteenth-century France and to the pre-Christian traditions of ancient Greece, Hinduism and Taoism.

Weil's concept of mysticism was inextricably bound with intellectual effort. However, she was careful to distinguish between what she called 'attention' and mere application of effort. Attention requires a kind of focused detachment, creation of a state in which the mind is floating – ready for penetration by truth. Her description overlaps or echoes the concentrative meditation practised by the yogis of Eastern religions, whom Weil greatly admired. Because of this emphasis on attention, sustained 'without regard for results', Weil concludes that even atheism can lead directly to spiritual truth – hinting that she does not perceive her own change in direction as a radical departure:

> Not to believe in the immortality of the soul, but to look upon the whole of life as destined to prepare for the moment of death; not to believe in God, but to love the universe, always, even in the throes of anguish, as a home – there lies the road toward faith by way of atheism. This is the same faith as that which shines resplendent in religious symbols. But when it is reached by this road, such symbols are of no practical use at all. (Weil, 1970, p. 308)

> Whatever a person's professed belief in regard to religious matters including atheism, wherever there is complete, authentic and unconditional consent to necessity, there is fullness of love for God; and nowhere else. This consent constitutes participation in the Cross of Christ. (Weil, 1957, p. 184)

Weil became increasingly convinced that the ability to sustain tension – to hold two polar opposites in one's consciousness simultaneously – requires an almost superhuman effort. Her own life illustrates her thinking: her move toward the spiritual domain parallels her growing ability to live with opposites, with contradiction. When she comes to identify with Christ, she does so primarily in response to Christ's experience of contradiction, that is, with Christ on the cross, not the Christ resurrected: 'Contradiction experienced to the very depths of the being tears us heart and soul: it is the cross'

(Weil, 1951a, p. 89). In defining the cross as contradiction, Weil brings together coherently the themes of attention, looking versus eating, and reality-as-contradiction:

> All those who possess in its pure state the love of their neighbour and the acceptance of the order of the world, including affliction – all those, even should they live and die to all appearances atheists, are surely saved. (Weil, 1953, p. 36)

> Contact with the beauty of Christianity, presented simply as a beautiful thing to be savored, would imperceptibly imbue the mass of the population with spirituality, if it is still capable of being so imbued, far more effectively than any amount of dogmatic teaching of religious beliefs. (Weil, 1952, p. 93)

> [T]he proper function of religion . . . is to suffuse with its light all secular life, public or private, without ever in any way dominating it. (Weil, 1953, p. 36)

> Love for our neighbor, being made of creative attention, is analogous to genius. (Weil, 1951a, p. 149)

> I do not know whether Christ did or did not raise Lazarus from the dead. But if he actually did so, first, it was an action that he performed in his capacity as a man, like all those he performed on this earth, and secondly, this action was performed as the result of a perfectly intelligible mechanism for anyone capable of taking this mechanism to pieces. (Weil, 1956, p. 315)

> Hitler could die and return to life again fifty times, but I should still not look upon him as the Son of God. And if the Gospel omitted all mention of Christ's resurrection, faith would be easier for me. The Cross by itself suffices me. (Weil, 1953, p. 55)

> The reason why man cannot evade the religious problem is because he finds the opposition of good and evil an intolerable burden. It makes an atmosphere in which he cannot breathe. (Weil, 1962, p. 211)

According to Susan Taubes, 'Simone Weil has universalized the historical experience of the death of God into a theological principle. The unworldliness of God, his silence, and nothingness are his most essential features. God can be present to us only in the form of his absence' (Taubes, 1955, p. 6). Weil refused to seek comfort in religion, for she felt that this impulse obscured the true nature of the human condition. Consequently, Taubes proposes, Weil 'repudiates, point by point, the major dogmas of the church regarding resurrection, providence, immortality, miracles, and eschatology' (Taubes, 1955, p. 8). For Weil, humanity must attempt to imitate the acceptance of distance and incongruity, an act Christ performed by actively choosing the horror of the cross:

> There is no reason whatever to suppose that after so atrocious a crime as the murder of a perfect being humanity must needs have become better; and, in fact, taken in the mass, it does not appear to have done so. (Weil, 1953, p. 47)

> Christianity . . . when it first began, was dangerous to the established order. . . . It very quickly mended its ways, learnt how to make the proper distinction between the marriage and burial ceremonies for the rich and those for the poor, and to relegate the unfortunate to the back seats. (Weil, 1973, p. 145)

> Such a horrible thing as the crucifixion of Christ could only happen in a place in which evil very far outweighed good. But not only that, the Church, born and bred in such a place, must need be impure from the beginning and remain so. (Weil, 1953, p. 44)

> We must be happy in the knowledge that he [God] is infinitely beyond our reach. Thus we can be certain that the evil in us, even if it overwhelms our whole being, in no way sullies the divine purity, bliss, and perfection. (Weil, 1951a, p. 216)

> Christ offered up his life; but at the moment when death was near, his suffering did not appear to him as an offering; it filled him with horror, and he only accepted it as being the will of God. We don't imitate him by conforming to present-day customs. (Weil, 1956, p. 447)

> Mysticism means passing beyond the sphere where good and evil

are in opposition, and this is achieved by the union of the soul with the absolute good. (Weil, 1962, p. 214)

The Gospels are the last and most marvellous expression of Greek genius, as the *Iliad* is its first expression. (Weil, 1957, p. 52)

As with many mystics, Simone Weil's mystical experience heightened her struggle for social justice; the 'private' moment of illumination and a 'public' commitment to social change that ensues are not antithetical. In Weil's terms, what is required is a proper joining of thought with action. Although the mystic experience is ineffable, the need to communicate it is a constant. Further, the message communicated often reflects a questioning of the current social order, the 'world as it is'. As a result, the mystical vision is almost inevitably a subversive one:

The truly Christian inspiration has fortunately been preserved by mysticism. (Weil, 1952, p. 277)

One can say without fear of exaggeration that today the spirit of truth is almost absent from religious life. (Weil, 1952, p. 250)

[T]rue faith constitutes a very different form of adhesion from that which consists in believing such-and-such an option. The whole notion of faith then needs to be thought out anew. (Weil, 1953, pp. 46–7)

Christianity is, in effect, apart from a few isolated centers of inspiration, something socially in accordance with the interests of those who exploit the people. (Weil, 1952, p. 248)

Besides, it is written that the tree shall be known by its fruits. The Church has borne too many evil fruits for there not to have been some mistake made at the beginning. (Weil, 1953, p. 31)

I am well aware that the Church must inevitably be a social structure; otherwise it would not exist. But in so far as it is a social structure, it belongs to the Prince of this World. (Weil, 1951a, p. 54)

Simone Weil's mystical experiences could be construed as adaptive regressions that she seems to have integrated successfully with the rest of her life and work. Her first such experience was triggered by a poem pertaining to eating; much of her work uses eating as a metaphor for refusing to close gaps prematurely even when one desires to do so; and her death occurs simultaneously with a refusal to eat. From the vantage point of Weil herself, her mystical experiences are consistent with her entire life and work, differing from other life experiences primarily in their intensity and authenticity:

> Whereas what is really marvellous, in the case of the mystics and the saints, is not that they have more life, a more intense life than that of other people, but that in them truth should have become life. (Weil, 1952, p. 249)

Decreation
Denial of Self

Commentators who conclude that Weil's life was a failure, without specifying the criteria by which such a judgement is reached, ignore important questions. In many instances, they have simply assumed goal-oriented criteria and then applied those to Weil, a person whose life and work hinged upon a theme of seeking knowledge and experience *without regard for results*. No wonder, then, that Weil felt so misunderstood: 'They content themselves with uttering a few eulogistic epithets . . . they listen to me or read me with the same fleeting attention they give everything else. . . . They haven't tired themselves' (Weil, 1978, pp. 1–2). The problem, of course, is how to arrive at a valuation of the work of a young woman who died at the age of thirty-four in a sanatorium, seemingly by her own choosing. The irony is that some of those who label her death as suicide, moral masochism or self-destruction worship a young man who died at almost the same age, in a manner he too could have avoided.

Decreating the self

The reciprocal relationship between God's creative action in the world and human participation in creation is a crucial one for Simone Weil. She asserts that God's part in creation 'is not an act of self-expansion but of restraint and renunciation' (Weil, 1951a, p. 145). Weil sees what she termed 'decreation' as a response to God's act of creation. Through the act of creation, God allowed something other than itself to exist, and therefore in the act of renouncing the 'I', or 'decreating' the self, the individual acknowledges oneness with God. According to Weil, 'God created me as non-being appearing to exist, so that, by renouncing through love this apparent existence, I may be annihilated in the fullness of being' (Weil, 1950, p. 42). For Weil, human beings participate in the creative act through renunciation. Indeed, she interprets the supreme religious act as the completion of self-denial, 'decreation' of the self. Susan Taubes describes Weil's concept of decreation as 'a process of uprooting one's self, of accepting and loving the affliction that tears the soul from its social and vital attachments' (Taubes, 1955, p. 10). In Weil's understanding, the act of Christ dying on the cross, and doing so willingly, represents a perfect case of decreation. In believing that 'God has given me my being and at the same time the possibility of giving him something in return by ceasing to be', Weil concludes that 'by fatigue, affliction, and death, man is made matter and is consumed by God' (Weil, 1951a, p. 99). This notion is consistent with the fairy tale that so moved her as a young child: the heroine who chooses to enter the house by way of the door in tar receives gold, while the stepsister who chooses the golden door receives tar. Understanding Simone Weil's death is essential to interpreting her life, a task best undertaken through the crucial concept of decreation:

> [The way to truth is through one's own annihilation.] It is a state of extreme humiliation, and it is impossible for anyone who cannot accept humiliation.

Genius is the supernatural virtue of humility in the domain of thought. (Weil, 1970, p. 335)

The union of contradictories involves a wrenching apart. It is impossible without extreme suffering. (Weil, 1963, p. 92)

Christ was afflicted. He did not die like a martyr. He died like a common criminal, confused with thieves, only a little more ridiculous. For affliction is ridiculous. (Weil, 1951a, p. 125)

It is the absence of prestige, and not the physical suffering, which is the essence of the Passion. (Weil, 1957, p. 137)

Contradiction experienced to the very depths of the being tears us heart and soul: it is the cross. (Weil, 1963, p. 89)

The bringing about of the absence of God in a soul completely emptied of self through love is redemptive suffering. (Weil, 1963, p. 24)

What is generally named egoism is not love of self, it is a defect of perspective. (Weil, 1957, p. 133)

If I am sad, it comes primarily from the permanent sadness that destiny has imprinted forever upon my emotions, where the greatest and purest joys can only be superimposed and that at the price of a great effort of attention. (Weil, 1977, p. 21)

Weil understands decreation as a way of being or standing in the world; it is an orientation within and toward life. Weil assumes that to experience life fully one must be willing to empty the self by way of attention, then allow the self to be filled by remaining in a state of waiting. The capacity to live life fully, to embrace all of reality as it presents itself, necessarily requires that the self be permeable. As human beings progress through life, all of the tactics, manoeuvres, defences and strategies that they employ to reduce the likelihood of pain, hurt or disappointment bring with them an unintended side effect: they simultaneously limit the level of fulfilment (filling of the self) that humans may experience in exact proportion to the amount of protection from harm that the mechanisms of defence afford.

When an intimate relationship that once was intense, meaningful and highly valued comes to an end in unexpected hurt and despair, one of the most common tactics is withdrawal: in order to avoid experiencing such depth of pain and hurt again, never allow anyone to come close again. Weil would agree that such a strategy succeeds in protecting a person from suffering, but she would warn that it has a high price, because the same boundaries that protect the self may serve as barriers to positive experiences. And because people never experience what could have been, they seldom learn the price paid for self-protection. In examining how much of life people choose to give up, Weil insisted that the search for truth and reality necessarily involves the risk of passing through tumultuous and painful experiences. Simone Weil put herself at both physical and emotional risk, recognizing this stance as essential to any quest for genuine truth:

> To acknowledge the reality of affliction means saying to oneself: 'I may lose at any moment, through the play of circumstances over which I have no control, anything whatsoever that I possess, including those things which are so intimately mine that I consider them as being myself. There is nothing that I might not lose. It could happen at any moment that what I am might be abolished and replaced by anything whatsoever of the filthiest and most contemptible sort.'
> To be aware of this in the depth of one's soul is to experience nonbeing. It is the state of extreme and total humiliation which is also the condition for passing over into truth. (Weil, 1977, p. 332)

> If we want to have a love which will protect the soul from wounds, we must love something other than God. (Weil, 1977, p. 358)

In the face of such descriptions, one may question whether Weil's approach is at all realistic. If everyone chose to follow the path advocated by Weil, what would life be like? Is there a difference between what Weil calls decreation and what most

people might call self-destruction? The answers to such important questions become more complex and less certain if life is
viewed without its final outcome in mind. Suppose, for instance,
that Weil did not die in a sanatorium at the age of thirty-four.
Instead, imagine that her text outlining steps for the reconstruction of France was published in 1944 (five years earlier
than the actual date) and hailed as an important document for
the country, one that her compatriots set about to implement.
Imagine that in 1948 (five years later than the actual date) she
died in a hospital from tuberculosis, after struggling valiantly
against the ravages of the disease. Even assuming that everything else in her life remained the same and every word that
she wrote were unchanged, the assessment of Simone Weil's
life and work would certainly be radically different. To assess a
life *only* by virtue of its outcome sidesteps significant themes in
the process of living, and it overlooks the crucial fact that people
live their lives forward, making numerous choices where they
do not and cannot predict the outcome or end product. In like
manner, the focus on outcomes also skews perceptions of the
rest of an individual's life; we explain, or 'explain away', based
on knowledge of the outcome.

With these provisos in mind, what can be said about the
'healthiness' of Weil's life path? Fredén (1982) argues that
mental health is secured by maintaining balance, equilibrium,
homeostasis. In contrast, any approach to life that upsets a balanced state, especially between need and fulfilment, makes the
individual vulnerable to conditions of hurt by creating a gap
between desires, expectations and results. The experience of
such a discrepancy is both the source of the imbalance and the
cause of pain. Therefore, the remedy for persons who experience this dissonance is to learn to cope, in ways reflected in
such colloquial phrases as 'lower your sights', 'be realistic',
'moderation in all things'. By these homeostatic standards of
mental health, Simone Weil must certainly be viewed as a failure. Weil not only refused to avoid gaps, she fervently sought

them. Her fundamental notions of *looking* and *eating* explicitly focus on intentionally maintaining a gap between need (desire) and its fulfilment, an arena that thinkers like Fredén see as especially crucial to mental health. Weil understands the urge to live within a normal curve of experience, but she also understands that the price for such a choice may be high. For one thing, coping refers to a set of techniques that change *only* the person; an individual *adjusts* to the world as it is. As people come to view life as continuous coping they lose an ability to perceive that 'such have we *made* the world.' Perhaps one of the most important aspects of her life is its ability to draw our attention to the often ignored costs of living with a simple focus on the process of coping.

In addition to ignoring the constructed nature of social reality, admonitions to 'be realistic' beg the most basic questions concerning what *is* 'realistic'. Recommending such coping strategies often assumes a simple outcome-based evaluation, only to overlook a fundamental attribute of human experience: it unfolds in time, as well as in space. When people embark on a life path, they do not know what the outcome will be, so how can they know in advance whether a particular goal is achievable or not? For example, is it 'realistic' to believe that it is possible to eliminate hunger in the world (as Gandhi believed) or to devote one's energies to achieving a clean, healthy environment (as many ecological activists have done)? Likewise, is it unrealistic to believe in a transcendent 'something more' that draws us upward by *grace* (as Simone Weil believed)?

Weil's decreation moves in the opposite direction from coping. By decreating her self, Simone Weil sought to remove the layers of cultural conditioning and shared illusions built up over a short lifetime, and she hungered for righteousness – politically, religiously and socially. She chose a life devoted to careful and accurate perception of reality, by way of attention and regardless of outcome. Mystics and existentialists alike have distinguished between a false self (the social self as an accidental by-product of conditioning) and an authentic self (that which remains once the conditioned layers of culture and circumstance are removed by conscious choice). Why do so few people seek the high standards of perceptual acuity and intellectual rigour that Weil herself sought? Perhaps her life offers the best reply. The answer, it seems, is one of cost. Readers of Weil may focus primarily on the outcome of her life because doing so reminds them of the potential cost of such a life course. However, if one remembers Simone Weil's own criterion – that one must choose a life of attention without regard for results – then her life is a model not of failure but of near perfection.

Bibliography

1. Works by Simone Weil

La Connaissance surnaturelle (1950) Paris: Gallimard. These notebooks contain entries that seem to have been written in 1942, following a period of grief and inability to write. Themes include Weil's analysis of the relationship between God and the individual and it includes some of her most melancholy pleas for spiritual understanding.

Waiting for God. (1951a) Trans. E. Crauford. New York: Harper & Row. This work is addressed to Father Perrin, and his introduction provides his view of Weil's rationale for not joining the Catholic Church. In a series of essays and letters, Weil critiques institutionalized religion, pointing out how the worldly manifestation differs from her conception of true religion.

La Condition ouvrière (1951b) Paris: Gallimard. These notebooks were written during her time as a factory worker, and they contain illustrations, spiritual musings and practical suggestions and analysis of how to make manufacturing more productive and humane. Although some of her ideas sound utopian – such as long, paid sabbatical voyages around the countryside for workers – a few of her suggestions for empowering workers and enhancing their sense of worth and ownership have become realities in some contemporary manufacturing companies.

The Need for Roots: Prelude to a Declaration of Duties Toward Mankind (1952) Trans. A. Wills. New York: Harper & Row. T.S. Eliot's effusive introduction to this work is almost solely responsible for bringing Weil to whatever public attention she has received. In this work Weil explains how she believes Europe should be restructured, attempting to convince the French Resistance that in order to truly defeat Nazism, a government must be just, rooted in spiritual values, and grounded as well in the physical well-being of all citizens.

Letter to a Priest (1953) London: Routledge & Kegan Paul. This is an auto-biographical letter to Father Perrin, in which she describes her first experiences of affliction as a factory worker. Here she recounts candidly the sense she had of being marked as a slave from that period onward.

The Notebooks of Simone Weil (1940–42) (1956) Trans. A. Wills. New York: G.P. Putnam's. These notebooks, written at the start of the war, contain analysis of the nature of oppression within the larger context of European history.

Intimations of Christianity among the Ancient Greeks (1957) Trans. Elizabeth Chase Geissbuhler. London: Routledge & Kegan Paul. This collection includes her analysis of the *Iliad* as a classic representation of the consequence of force, along with essays arguing that the roots of Christianity are to be found in Plato's writing. Weil also considers the spiritual dimensions of Pythagorean statements, elucidating connections between physical and mystical understanding of the universe.

Selected Essays (1934–43) (1962) Trans. Richard Rees. London: Oxford University Press. These essays range from discussions of Hitler to Weil's theories of human personality and her discussion of the Cathars' Languedoc society. It constitutes a varied and balanced collection from early to later work.

Gravity and Grace (1963) Arranged and introduced by G. Thibon. London: Routledge & Kegan Paul. Opening with an insightful and sympathetic introduction by Gustave Thibon, the man who provided her with the chance to carry out agricultural work, this collection of thoughts represents a mode of expression Weil first practised with her teacher, Alain. Some of these selections from the notebooks are extended essays on such topics as physical necessity and the impulse toward goodness, and others take the form of epigrams.

Seventy Letters (1965) Trans. Richard Rees. London: Oxford University Press. In some ways, this small selection gives one of the most intimate portraits of Weil, demonstrating how she addressed everyone from factory owners to her own closest friends with the same earnest seriousness and the same intense degree of intellectual rigour. A few letters reveal insecurities and regrets – a personal side of Weil which she struggled to efface from most of her writings.

On Science, Necessity, and the Love of God (1968) Collected and translated by R. Rees. London: Oxford University Press. Divided in two parts, this work includes her writings on mechanics, science, and on God.

First and Last Notebooks (1933–4, 1942–3) (1970) Trans. R. Rees. London: Oxford University Press. This collection of notebook entries features material from many of Weil's early lectures in philosophy in which she outlines her critique of Marxist materialism. Later entries include her responses to life in exile in New York, while the final entries are written during her time in London, when she was hoping to return to France.

Oppression and Liberty (1973) Trans. A. Wills and J. Petrie. Amherst: University of Massachusetts Press. Representing her most astute political thinking, this work addresses Marxist concepts of alienated labour, materialism, determinism, and Lenin's *Materialism and Empiriocriticism*. While supporting many of the aims of orthodox Marxism, she views the methods and emphasis on power as intrinsically corrupt.

The Simone Weil Reader (1977) Ed. G.A. Panichas. New York: David McKay. This anthology contains a wide range of Weil's work, including a letter published in *Politics* ('What is a Jew?'). The collection also includes essays from *Waiting on God, On Science, Necessity and the Love of God*, and two poems first published in the *Phoenix* and translated by William Burford. There are also some selections from *The Need for Roots, Gravity and Grace*, and her notebooks.

Lectures on Philosophy (1978) Notes of her lectures taken by A. Reynaud-Guérithault, trans. H. Price. Cambridge: Cambridge University Press.

Introduced by Peter Winch, this set of lecture notes taken by lycée pupil Anne Reynaud encapsulates her analysis of ontological questions.

Formative Writings (1929–1941) (1987) Ed. and trans. D.T. McFarland and W. van Ness. Amherst: University of Massachusetts Press. This set of writings begins with Weil's thesis on Descartes, published in France in the collection *Sur la Science* (1966). The work also contains her writing on factory experiences, published originally in *La Condition ouvrière* (1951b) by Gallimard. Here she offers her most specific remedies to the problems faced by working people.

2. Secondary works on Simone Weil

Allen, D. (1983) *Three Outsiders: Pascal, Kierkegaard, Simone Weil.* Cambridge, MA: Cowley Publications. Allen attempts to explain each of these philosophers' path to God. Although Allen has little political consciousness (note his title, with only Weil requiring a first name) and he may skew some of the philosophy to fit his own theological prejudices, he provides some interesting and valid comparisons and contrasts among the three thinkers.

Allen, L. (1976) French intellectuals and T.E. Lawrence. *Durham University Journal*, December: 52–66. This brief article includes a letter from Simone Weil to T.E. Lawrence, outlining what she feels constitutes human heroism. Rarely does Weil wax as effusive or personal as she does in this letter, and for this the article is worth reading.

Anderson, D. (1971) *Simone Weil.* London: SCM Press. A short but extremely useful text on Weil that places her writings within the context of her life's experiences. Anderson provides astute connections between historical and social circumstances and philosophical and intellectual developments in Weil's life.

Cliff, M. (1993) Sister/outsider: some thoughts on Simone Weil. In C. Ascher, L. De Salvo and S. Ruddick (eds), *Between Women*. London: Routledge. A tribute to Weil's personal and artistic influence, written from a deliberately subjective viewpoint, as part of a collection of essays and memoirs about famous women.

Blum, L.A. and Seidler, V.J. (1989) *A Truer Liberty: Simone Weil and Marxism*. New York: Routledge. Part of a series on critical social thought from the University of Wisconsin, which elucidates Weil's unique contribution to a form of political radicalism that simultaneously rejected traditional Marxism and its alternative, capitalist liberalism. The authors detail Weil's political activism, her critiques of Marxist and liberal conceptions of liberty, the Kantian sources of her analysis of oppression, the relationship between her work experience and her turn toward Christianity, her analysis of power relationships, and possible connections between her brand of religious and political activism and recent movements in Poland, liberation theology in Europe and Latin American, and Catholic radicalism in the United States and France.

Cabaud, J. (1964) *Simone Weil: A Fellowship in Love*. London: Harvill. This was the first major biography of Simone Weil, while a subsequent work by Cabaud (1967), *Simone Weil à New York et à Londres*, contains more information on Weil's later life but was never translated into English. Cabaud's work contains photographs and New York and London interviews, and his writings on Weil offer some insights not available in translated biographies.

Coles, R. (1987) *Simone Weil: A Modern Pilgrimage*. Reading, MA: Addison-Wesley. A look at Weil's life and some of the more difficult aspects of her philosophy, written with a religious focus.

Dietz, M.G. (1987) *Between the Human and the Divine: The Political Thought of Simone Weil*. Totowa, NJ: Rowman & Littlefield. A text designed to introduce Weil's social and political thought to scholarly criticism by examining and presenting her central arguments. Dietz demonstrates psychological, literary and political savvy in her critically sophisticated deconstructive analysis of Weil's thought.

Dunaway, J. (1984) *Simone Weil*. Boston: Twayne Publishers. Written from the perspective of one who considers Weil as a 'unique blend of rigid intellectual discipline and profound human compassion', this text includes biographical information as well as discussion of Weil's favourite topics.

Dunaway, J. (1985) Estrangement and the need for roots: prophetic visions of the human condition in Albert Camus and Simone Weil. *Religion and Literature*, *17* (2): 35–42. In a cogent literary analysis of Camus and

Weil, Dunaway argues that Weil's analysis offers at least as much insight into the human condition as her more famous compatriot, Albert Camus.

Fiori, G. (1989) *Simone Weil: An Intellectual Biography.* Athens, GA: University of Georgia Press. A biography that includes commentary from Weil's contemporaries and that provides a description of her social environment. This work aims to trace connections between her intellectual and personal values, but it does not always succeed in giving a coherent analysis of her writing.

Frost, C.J. (1980) On Simone Weil: self, God and world. *Reflections: Essays in Phenomenology, 1*: 27–38. This essay looks at the philosophy of Simone Weil from a psychological viewpoint, noting that artistic or mystical temperaments are often termed 'abnormal' by the social-scientific community. Frost suggests a reassessment of the categories and criteria used to determine individual worth in society.

Hellman, J. (1982) *Simone Weil: An Introduction to her Thought.* Philadelphia: Fortress Press. A study of Weil as an altruistic teacher with particular attention given to those qualities that separate her from other thinkers. Hellman distinguishes Weil's argument for rootedness from the religious and patriotic declarations to French citizens made by Maritain, De Gaulle and others. He also contrasts the vein of mysticism Weil advocates with the thought of other contemporary French writers on mysticism, such as Teilhard de Chardin and Denis de Rougemont.

Little, J.P. (1988) *Simone Weil: Waiting on Truth.* Oxford: Berg. A work that exposes the breadth of Weil's interests and the integration of her thought into her life. This work is useful in its comparison of Weil's thought with universal elements of mystical thought.

McFarland, D.T. (1983) *Simone Weil.* New York: Frederick Ungar. A compact work showing connections between Weil's cultural studies and her understanding of philosophy and history. McFarland interprets Weil's spiritual writings in a non-religious context, in an effort to counteract what she views as a heavy emphasis on Weil as a spokesperson for more orthodox Christianity.

McLane-Iles, B. (1986) *Uprooting and Integration in the Writings of Simone Weil.* New York: Peter Lang. Part of a series of American University

Studies on Theology and Religion. McLane-Iles takes a deconstructionist approach to Weil's thought, looking at her rejection of Cartesian solipsism, her critiques of materialist and idealist approaches to perception and knowledge, as well as her deconstruction of the concepts of power, science and self, and her reintegration of meaning. She offers a useful explanation of Weil's theory that our culture places the most value on literary works that emphasize force and victory.

McLellan, D. (1990) *Utopian Pessimist: The Life and Thought of Simone Weil.* New York: Poseidon Press. This work provides an introduction to the life and thought of Weil and information about the influences that affected her perspective. Although McLellan includes biographical information, he places more emphasis on Weil's contributions to the study of comparative theology, philosophy, cultural studies and sociology.

Milosz, C. (1977) *Emperor of the Earth: Modes of Eccentric Vision.* Berkeley, CA: University of California Press. In the chapter, 'The Importance of Simone Weil', Milosz describes Weil as a Christian who was willing to incorporate Greek thought, history, science and politics into a belief system that recognized the importance of human suffering.

Nye, A. (1994) *Philosophia: The Thought of Rosa Luxemburg, Simone Weil, and Hannah Arendt.* London: Routledge. Nye presents the philosophies of these three great women thinkers and investigates in detail the differences between their modes of thinking and those of their male counterparts. This analysis provides insight into female perspectives on the human condition and elucidates the major philosophical issues considered by feminist scholars in the twentieth century.

Oldfield, S. (1989) *Women against the Iron Fist: Alternatives to Militarism 1900–1989.* Oxford: Basil Blackwell. Chapters and sections devoted to Weil situate her pacifist thought in the midst of women's peace movements of the day. This analysis provides a useful history of pacifist women's activities in Europe and the United States.

Perrin, J.M. and Thibon, G. (1953) *Simone Weil As We Knew Her.* London: Routledge & Kegan Paul. A Catholic appraisal of Weil by friends who knew her well and to whom she entrusted the bulk of her writings. Joseph Marie Perrin was a Dominican priest with whom Weil often argued, and Gustave Thibon was a farmer and lay theologian who helped her find work in the Ardèche vineyards. Their work is at once candid in describing the thorniness of her personality and imbued with deep admiration for her spiritual quest.

Petrément, S. (1976) *Simone Weil: A Life*. Trans. Raymond Rosenthal. New York: Pantheon Books. A biography written by a close friend of Weil's, this book reveals the connections between Weil's experiences and her studies. Unlike other texts which elevate Weil to virtual sainthood, this book unveils the human at the centre of the divine thinking.

Rees, R. (1958) *Brave Men: A Study of D.H. Lawrence and Simone Weil*. Carbondale: Southern Illinois University Press. This work, closely connected with the biography, offers comparisons between the mysticism of Lawrence and that of Weil.

Rees, R. (1966) *Simone Weil: A Sketch for a Portrait*. Carbondale: Southern Illinois University Press. In this biography, Rees stresses the individuality of Weil's thought. Richard Rees translated Weil's writing and authored works on her that deal equally with religious and political issues. In colourful language, Rees attempts a balanced portrait of Weil, whom he notes 'is all too easy for any biographer to dramatise . . . as a sort of St. Joan of the Workshops or to sentimentalise . . . as an up-to-date blend of Hypatia and the Little Flower' (p. 11).

Reynaud-Guérithault, A. (listed as Weil, 1978) *Simone Weil: Lectures on Philosophy*, trans. H. Price. Cambridge: Cambridge University Press. An interesting account of Weil's philosophy, based on the personal experience of a former student. This collection of lecture notes provides a different slant on Weil, including information and ideas that are missing in her other published work. However, readers should not lose sight of the fact that the lecture notes are those of Reynaud-Guérithault, not the original notes from which Weil lectured.

Sontag, S. (1978/1982) *Against Interpretation and Other Essays*. New York: Octagon Books. Susan Sontag devotes a piece to Weil in her collection of essays on varied subjects, in which she examines how one may view the example of Weil's life with both sympathetic puzzlement for her masochism and admiration for her heroism.

Springsted, E.O. (1986) *Simone Weil and the Suffering of Love*. Cambridge, MA: Cowley Publications. A Christian interpretation of Weil's philosophy, this work attempts to place her closer to mainstream, orthodox

Christianity. It draws heavily on the accounts of her theological companions, Perrin and Thibon.

Springsted, E.O. (1989) The religious basis of culture: T.S. Eliot and Simone Weil. *Religious Studies*, *25* (1): 105–16. Springsted observes that Weil offers a more complete understanding of how to establish rootedness through labour in *The Need for Roots* than Eliot does in his two monographs, *The Idea of a Christian Society* and *Notes Towards the Definition of Culture*.

Strickland, S. (1993) *The Red Virgin: A Poem of Simone Weil*. Madison: University of Wisconsin Press. Winner of the Brittingham Prize in Poetry, this collection of short poems covers the main areas of Weil's life and thought, and they include some 'found' poems, such as letters from Weil's mother or entries on Weil in Simone de Beauvoir's notebooks. The purity, renunciation of physical pleasure and acceptance of suffering that accompanied her quest receive tribute in this book. Illustrating a keen understanding of Weil's life and work, Strickland reminds the reader that her collection of poems is really one poem – just as the myriad themes that Weil addresses and lives are united in her one brief life.

Taubes, S.A. (1955) The absent God. *Journal of Religion*, *35* (1): 6–16. This article offers an insightful analysis of Weil's attempt to identify an absent, non-comforting God. Although this work makes Weil's thought accessible to agnostic or atheist readers, it distorts her vision by eliminating large portions of her work in favour of a focus on the darker elements of Weil's worldview.

Terry, M. (1973) *Approaching Simone*. Old Westbury, NY: The Feminist Press. This play, written in the avant-garde personal and political style typical of Megan Terry, highlights the salient features of Weil's political and ethical belief system. It also sensationalizes the psychological dimensions of Weil's life, but it does so in a way that creates a saintly portrait of Weil.

Tomlin, E.W.F. (1954) *Simone Weil*. Cambridge, MA: Bowes & Bowes. This short text reveals biographical information and establishes the historical and philosophical context within which Weil wrote. This work contains information not found in many of the longer biographies and is therefore worth a look.

West, P. (1966) *The Wine of Absurdity: Essays on Literature and Consolation.* University Park, PA: Pennsylvania State University Press. West discusses the synthesis in Weil's religious thought as well as her search for mystical enlightenment. Writing from a religious viewpoint, West nevertheless maintains some even-handedness in his portrait of Weil's thought.

White, G.A. (1981) *Simone Weil: Interpretations of a Life.* Amherst: University of Massachusetts Press. An anthology of essays on Weil with topics including biographical information, politics and scholarly criticism. This is one of the most thought-provoking and politically nuanced works on Weil, approaching her work from a variety of perspectives, including that of a revolutionary labour leader and a feminist scholar. M. Murray's 'The jagged edge: a biographical essay on Simone Weil' explores her origins and influence using the methods of 'new historicism' by attempting to identify the periods of her popularity, placing her within the historical context, and deconstructing a figure whom most previous authors treated with reverential awe. R. Coles provides a brief paean to her mission to find truth, and J.M. Cameron calls on readers to address the validity of her ultimate mission – enlightenment or death. In 'Simone Weil: last things', Murray movingly examines Weil's last days, imagining the activities and mindset of Weil in her final months and hours of life. M.K. Ferber criticizes the limitations and lacunae in Weil's interpretation of the *Iliad*, nevertheless concluding that her insights on the nature of force and the automatism of violence constitute valuable contributions, while J.H. Summers defends her interpretation as being primarily a document for its time, never intended to serve as a complete analysis of the *Iliad*. C.C. O'Brien, a politician, comments on her work from a political perspective, and Staughton Lynd views her as a member of the 'First New Left'. G.A. White offers an elucidating account of Weil's experiences with manual labour, comparing them with those of George Orwell and Dorothy Day – neither of whom had the extensive immersion experienced by Weil.

References

Addelson, K. (1987) Moral passages. In E.F. Kittay and D.T. Meyers (eds), *Women and Moral Theory*. Totowa, NJ: Rowman and Littlefield.

Arnold, G.L. (1951) Simone Weil. *Cambridge Journal, 4*, 6: 333–38.

Ascher, C., DeSalvo, L. and Ruddick, S. (eds) (1993) *Between Women: Biographers, Novelists, Critics, Teachers and Artists Write About Their Work on Women*. New York: Routledge.

Buber, M. (1952) *Good and Evil*. New York: Charles Scribner's Sons.

Buber, M. (1970) *I and Thou*. New York: Charles Scribner's Sons.

Cameron, J.M. (1981) The life and death of Simone Weil. In G.A. White (ed.), *Simone Weil*. Amherst: University of Massachusetts Press.

Cliff, M. (1993) Sister/outsider: some thoughts on Simone Weil. In C. Ascher, L. DeSalvo and S. Ruddick (eds) *Between Women: Biographers, Novelists, Critics, Teachers and Artists Write About Their Work on Women*. New York: Routledge.

Coles, R. (1987) *Simone Weil: A Modern Pilgrimage*. Reading, MA: Addison-Wesley.

De Beauvoir, S. (1958) *Mémoires d'une jeune fille rangée*. Paris: Gallimard.

Dietz, M.G. (1987) *Between the Human and the Divine: The Political Thought of Simone Weil*. Totowa, NJ: Rowman and Littlefield.

Dunaway, J. (1985) Estrangement and the need for roots: prophetic visions of the human condition in Albert Camus and Simone Weil. *Religion and Literature, 17*, 2: 35–42.

Ellmann, M. (1993) *The Hunger Artists: Starving, Writing, and Imprisonment*. Cambridge, MA: Harvard University Press.

Fiedler, L. (1951) Simone Weil: prophet out of Israel, saint of the absurd. *Commentary*, January: 36–46.

Fiori, G. (1989) *Simone Weil: An Intellectual Biography*. Athens, GA: University of Georgia Press.

Fredén, L. (1982) *Psychosocial Aspects of Depression: No Way Out?* New York: Wiley.

Gregory, J. (1990) A letter to Simone Weil. *Cross Currents, 40*, 3: 368–85.

Haskins, C.H. (1927) *The Renaissance of the Twelfth Century*. Cambridge, MA: Harvard University Press.

Hellman, J. (1982) *Simone Weil: An Introduction to her Thought*. Philadephia: Fortress Press.

Henle, M. (1978) One man against the Nazis – Wolfgang Köhler. *American Psychologist, 33*: 939–51.

Hirsch, A. (1981) *The New French Left: An Intellectual History from Sartre to Gorz*. Boston: South End Press.

Irigaray, L. (1985) *Speculum of the Other Woman*, trans. G.C. Gill. Ithaca, NY: Cornell University Press.

James, W. (1890/1950) *The Principles of Psychology*, 2 vols. New York: Dover.

Langer, S. (1942) *Philosophy in a New Key*. Cambridge, MA: Harvard University Press.

Little, J.P. (1988) *Simone Weil: Waiting on Truth*. Oxford: Berg.

Lugones, M. and Spelman, E. (1983) Have we got a theory for you! In *Hypatia* (special issue of Women's Studies International Forum), *6*, 6: 573–81.

McFarland, D.T. (1983) *Simone Weil*. New York: Frederick Ungar.

McLellan, D. (1990) *Utopian Pessimist: The Life and Thought of Simone Weil*. New York: Poseidon Press.

Merleau-Ponty, M. (1962) *Phenomenology of Perception*. Atlantic Highlands, NJ: Humanities.

Murray, M. (1973) The passion of Simone Weil. *Cross Currents, 23*: 213–218.

Nye, A. (1994) *Philosophia: The Thought of Rosa Luxemburg, Simone Weil, and Hannah Arendt*. London: Routledge.

Oldfield, S. (1989) *Women against the Iron Fist: Alternatives to Militarism 1900–1989*. Oxford: Basil Blackwell.

Perrin, J.M. and Thibon, G. (1953) *Simone Weil As We Knew Her*. London: Routledge & Kegan Paul.

Pétrement, S. (1976) *Simone Weil: A Life*, trans. R. Rosenthal. New York: Pantheon Books.

Rees, R. (1966) *Simone Weil: A Sketch for a Portrait*. Carbondale: Southern Illinois University Press.

Rees, R. (1970) Preface. In Simone Weil, *First and Last Notebooks*, trans. R. Rees. London: Oxford University Press.

Robertson, M. (1992) *Starving in the Silences*. New York: New York University Press.

Springsted, E.O. (1986) *Simone Weil and the Suffering of Love*. Cambridge, MA: Cowley Publications.

Strickland, S. (1993) *The Red Virgin: A Poem of Simone Weil*. Madison: University of Wisconsin Press.

Taubes, S.A. (1955) The absent God. *Journal of Religion, 35*(1): 6–16.

Taylor, M. (1973) History, humanism and Simone Weil. *Commonweal, 24*: 448–52.

Terry, M. (1973) *Approaching Simone*. Old Westbury, NY: The Feminist Press.

Walker, M.U. (1992) Feminism, ethics, and the question of theory. *Hypatia, 7*, 3: 23–38.

Weil, S. (1950) *La Connaissance surnaturelle*. Paris: Gallimard.

Weil, S. (1951a) *Waiting for God*, trans. E. Crauford. New York: Harper & Row.

Weil, S. (1951b) *La Condition ouvrière*, Paris: Gallimard.

Weil, S. (1952) *The Need for Roots: Prelude to a Declaration of Duties toward Mankind*, trans. A. Wills. New York: Harper & Row.

Weil, S. (1953) *Letter to a Priest*. London: Routledge & Kegan Paul.

Weil, S. (1956) *The Notebooks of Simone Weil (1940–42)*, trans. A. Wills. New York: G.P. Putnam's Sons.

Weil, S. (1957) *Intimations of Christianity among the Ancient Greeks*, trans. E.C. Geissbuhler. London: Routledge & Kegan Paul.

Weil, S. (1962) *Selected Essays (1934–43)*, trans. R. Rees. London: Oxford University Press.

Weil, S. (1963) *Gravity and Grace*, arranged and introduced by G. Thibon. London: Routledge & Kegan Paul.

Weil, S. (1965) *Seventy Letters*, trans. R. Rees. London: Oxford University Press.

Weil, S. (1968) *On Science, Necessity, and the Love of God*, collected and translated by R. Rees. London: Oxford University Press.

Weil, S. (1970) *First and Last Notebooks (1933–4, 1942–3)*, trans. R. Rees. London: Oxford University Press.

Weil, S. (1973) *Oppression and Liberty*, trans. A. Wills and J. Petrie. Amherst: University of Massachusetts Press.

Weil, S. (1977) *The Simone Weil Reader*, ed. G.A. Panichas. New York: David McKay.

Weil, S. (1978) *Simone Weil: Lectures on Philosophy*. [Notes of her lectures taken by A. Reynaud-Guérithault, trans. H. Price.] Cambridge: Cambridge University Press.

Weil, S. (1981) Two Moral Essays: *Human Personality and On Human Obligations*. Wallingford, PA: Pendle Hill Publishing.

Weil, S. (1987) *Formative Writings: 1929–1941*, ed. and trans. D.T. McFarland and W. van Ness. Amherst: University of Massachusetts Press.

West, P. (1966) *The Wine of Absurdity: Essays on Literature and Consolation*. University Park, PA: Pennsylvania State University Press.

White, G.A. (1981) *Simone Weil: Interpretations of a Life*. Amherst: University of Massachusetts Press.

Index

DATE DUE

MAY - 7 2001

JUL - 7 2001

3 5282 0049

DEMCO 13829810

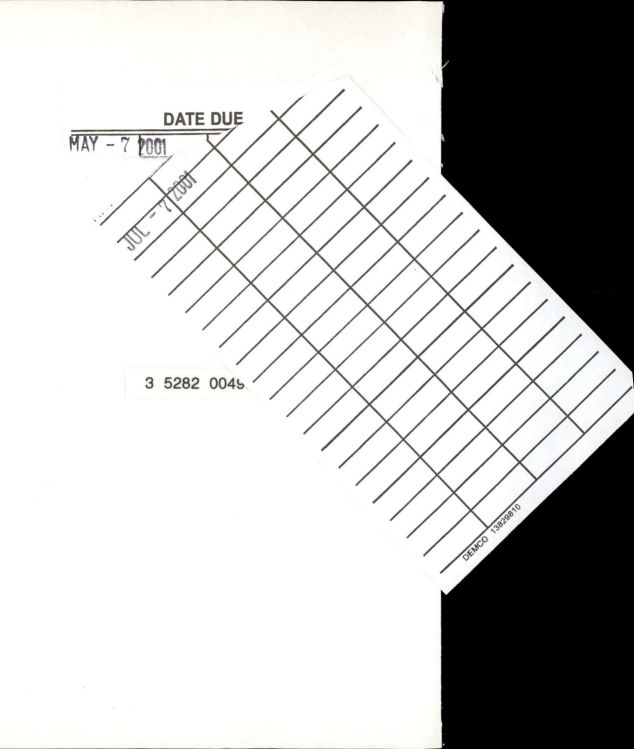